A Self-Help Guide for Copywriters

A resource for writing headlines and building creative confidence

Dan Nelken

Every effort has been made to trace or contact all copyright holders. The publishers
will be pleased to make good any omissions or rectify any mistakes brought to their
attention at the earliest opportunity.
First paperback edition December 2021
Book design by Sara Creative
ISBN 978-1-7777835-0-1 (paperback)
ISBN 978-1-7777835-1-8 (e-book)
www.nelkencreative.com

To you,
Create something you have complete control over.
It doesn't matter if it's perfect. All that matters is that it's yours.

(To Sara, Finn + Poppy, I love you times a zillion)

Ingredients

Section II: Headline Techniques

Section III: Types of Headlines

Section IV: This is Your Brain on Copywriting

Foreword

(Insert glowing review from the ad industry legend of your choice here)

Preface

I wrote *A Self-Help Guide for Copywriters* to help myself. I wrote the thing I wish I'd had at the beginning of my career, five years into my career, and last week. But that's not where this journey started for me.

A few years ago, I was having lunch with a friend, who at the time was creative director for a global brand. I mentioned toying with the idea of creating an online course about writing headlines. I explained the gist of my approach and went back to slurping my miso soup.

Part of me knew this course would be no different than the countless other ideas I'd had over the years. I'd talk about it for a while, get a few people to say, "That's great, Dan. Good for you," and then as soon as a newer, shinier idea came along, I'd toss it into the nearest dumpster.

Yet, here you are reading these words. And these three.

This is because a few hours post-miso, my friend emailed asking if I could teach this non-existent course to his creative department.

Uh-oh.

I sent a high estimate to scare him off.

"Can you also organize lunch?"

Uh-oh.

My estimate consisted of a three-hour session, plus a leave-behind in the form of a booklet thingy the writers could one day pass on to their copywriter grandchildren.

I had eight weeks to create a course and write this thingy, while working full time. One month in, it was sixty pages long with no end in sight. I hadn't even thought about the presentation deck. Or dietary preferences.

I decided to do what any rational human being would do in this situation — fake my own death and flee the country.

But before the glue had dried on my fake moustache, I caught a lucky break. My friend was let go (sorry, Chris) and my little course was headed right where it belonged — the nearest dumpster.

I was relieved because I liked my life in Canada but disappointed because in preparing for this course, I realized I needed it as much as anyone. I realized that throughout my career there had been little to no professional development focused on the craft of copywriting or creativity. I heard a lot of talk about the importance of "working on your craft," but there was little walk.

In the ad agencies I worked at, I was surrounded by hilarious and talented people and exposed to the world's greatest ads through award annuals. But there were zero resources put toward deliberately teaching and growing the team's craft.

For those of us privileged enough to go to an ad school, we developed a foundation and learned how hard we had to work (to do great work), but the intentional development ended when the career started. At least it did for me.

There's always going to be an element of sink or swim to start any career, but it's in every agency's best interest to proactively develop talent once someone's proven they can float. The fact there's little to no ongoing professional development for most creatives in advertising is batshit crazy for several reasons. Here are two biggies:

1. Creativity is our bread and butter
This industry prides itself on being at the forefront of creativity. But instead of creating conditions to help creativity flourish, it often does the opposite.

Many industries look for ways to create efficiencies in their work. But us, we're either too caught up in the busyness of our days or too proud to admit that a term like "efficiencies" could apply to creativity. And so, our answer is often working longer and harder. But what if we could find ways to get to better ideas, faster? As the demand for content grows and budgets and timelines shrink, this should be at the top of our to-do list.

And numero dos …

2. Creative self-doubt
Self-doubt, you know, the asshole inner voice that's always telling you you're not good enough? Yeah, that. I haven't met a half-decent creative who doesn't have that. And I've met many who were so impacted by it, it drove them out of the business altogether.

I think some degree of self-doubt is normal and can even be a motivator, but left unchecked, it can become paralyzing and impact more than your work. I've had to deal with it on almost every single brief. But in creating this book, I've become so much more aware of my process. The result has been a greater confidence in my abilities and a heightened level of self-awareness that allows me to whack-a-mole any self-doubting thoughts before their ugly little faces can take a breath.

It took me a while to admit I struggled with it but once I did, I was surprised to learn how many other people felt the same way. Yet still, most of the industry doesn't acknowledge it. Or we just accept that it comes with the territory and don't give it a second thought. Or maybe it's because it's tied to mental health and that's a subject we're all supposed to keep to ourselves. Feelings are for the weak. Whatever the reason, creative departments have to start getting proactive with helping employees build their craft. Otherwise, the work needlessly suffers, and so can people.

For these two ginormous reasons, I felt compelled to start down this path of helping people understand the creative process and become happier, healthier, and more confident.

Welcome to the course that became a booklet thingy that became a book. And might one day become a course.

Why the focus on headlines?

From aspiring to expiring copywriters, I kept noticing a lack of confidence in the craft of writing headlines, which is crazy because it's a huge part of our job. Some might say that is our job.

For me personally, this insecurity stemmed from being a writer in an industry that's been shifting more and more visual for over thirty years. I forced myself to think visually because that's what was valued. And I was consistently rewarded and awarded. But my writing muscles, if I had any to begin with, had atrophied.

Breaking down the craft of writing headlines has provided me with a foundation for all creative thinking and writing; from a headline on a billboard to a subject line in an email, or a witty line in an office birthday card.

So, what's in this book, and who's it for?

It's exclusively for copywriters. And also, for people who want to write like copywriters. It's a little about the creative process and a lot about the craft of writing headlines, including more than two hundred examples.

If you're looking for "killer headline formulas that can't fail," "data-driven headline conversion hacks," "SEO secrets (Google doesn't want you to know)," or "can't-miss clickbait headlines," you can find everything you need in a search bar. If you want to learn how to come up with a crap ton of ideas and turn them into headlines that bring personality to your writing and help you communicate like a human instead of a robot, this is the place to be.

If you're an experienced copywriter, some of this will feel familiar, but I've tried to break things down to be more actionable. Because knowing something isn't the same as doing it.

Oh, and as much as the title of this book, A Self-Help Guide for Copywriters, was meant to be a little tongue-in-cheek, it comes from a very authentic desire to help with the mental hurdles and blocks we face during the creative process. I've read several books on creativity in advertising, but I've yet to read one that addressed the subject of self-doubt directly.

I hope you learn half as much from reading this, as I did from writing it. And whether you're a copywriter or a normal person, that it gives you more confidence in your creative writing superpowers.

I could go on and on.

And I will. Because this is a book.

Note: This is also an excellent resource for people who dislike copywriters. Maybe you're a client, a designer, or even worse, in a relationship with a copywriter. Learn these tips and soon you'll be able to easily point out errors in their work and make the fragile copywriter in your life feel even more insecure.

Section I:
The Creative
Process

THE CREATIVE PROCESS

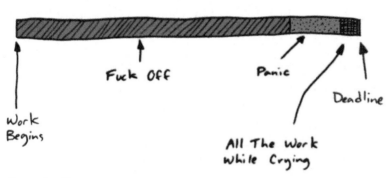

toothpastefordinner.com

When I first saw this meme, I laughed. Because it's true. But when I think about it, it's not funny at all. Because it's true.

As creatives, we resist structure. It's part of our identity as corporate rebels. Having no process or structure is what separates us from people who have to wear pants to work.

But what this no-process process can create is chaos. It's part of the reason we face so much self-doubt. How could you be confident if you don't know how you do what you do? This is also why imposter syndrome kicks in. When we don't know how we do what we do, every brief feels like the first. So, we work around the clock (calendar), hoping the advertising gods deliver in time for our presentations.

The time spent is a problem. But the most exhausting bit is all the time spent self-doubting and feeling like a fraud. It's punishing and it's cumulative. And we wonder why burnout is so common.

The good news, whether you want to admit it or not, is that you do have a process. There's a structure to creativity. It doesn't just happen. You have a way of solving problems; a pattern of thinking. You've just likely never thought about it. You've never broken it down. And because you're not aware of your process, it feels like you're playing the lottery every single time you have to write lines or come up with ideas.

> *"[T]he production of ideas is just as definite a process as the production of Fords; that the production of ideas, too, runs on an assembly line; that in this production the mind follows an operative technique which can be learned and controlled; and that its effective use is just as much a matter of practice in the technique as is the effective use of any tool."*

— James Webb Young, A Technique for Producing Ideas

I'm not expecting you to be a creative robot. You have to leave room in the process to think without structure. But by having a structure to lean on, even if it's just for when things get rough, you can start to turn chaos into confidence. This isn't math, but it's also not the witchcraft we make it out to be. And rather than being a constraint, structure can kick the door to creativity off its hinges.

By the end of this section, I'll cover the foundational structure for coming up with ideas, which you'll then be able to turn into headlines. Being familiar with this structure will give you more control over your work and help give those advertising gods a well-deserved break.

If you prefer the tortured artist route it's up to you, but if you think you might enjoy a life with less pain and more confidence...

Think First. Write Second.

The first mistake you can make when you have to write headlines is starting by writing headlines.

If you start with writing, you're starting with a blank page and a blank brain. And for every second that goes by without your brain spitting out a decent headline, the critic, that judgmental voice that lives inside your brain, starts to gain momentum.

Starting with headlines feels like the most direct route, but forcing out one headline at a time is not only less efficient, it can be torture because the longer it takes, the louder and more insulting your inner critic becomes. Repeat this process-less pattern enough, and before too long, you can start to believe the things it says.

So how do you shut it up?

You have to think before you write because great headlines aren't great sentences—they're great ideas expressed in words. Remember, you're a creative first and writer second.

Great headlines aren't great sentences—they're great ideas expressed in words.

If you want to write great headlines, the rule of thumb is—for every great one, you have to write a hundred. That's never going to be easy, but doing it without any structure makes it near impossible. Luke Sullivan, author of Hey, Whipple, Squeeze This, deserves most of the credit/blame for popularizing this rule. If writing a hundred headlines isn't intimidating enough, he clarifies: *"This is sitting down and slowly cranking out 100 workable lines—100 lines that range from decent, to hey-not-bad, to whoa-that-rocks. The key is they all have to be pretty good."*

So if the first step isn't writing, what is it? You come up with a whole schwack of ideas. And they become headline-writing springboards.

Create Your Buckets

Your first step to writing one hundred-plus headlines is coming up with all the different areas or buckets you can then ideate under.

These buckets should be simple, obvious places to start. If they're too obvious, you're on the right track. They aren't meant to be super deep or insightful. These are surface areas. Like digging for oil, you identify surface areas you think might lead to riches and then you drill into them. Your goal should be to find at least twenty. You'll find them by listing **benefits, attributes, insights, and truths** for whatever it is you're selling. Some of these areas won't bear fruit, or oil, but others...cha-ching.

When you start with buckets, your inner ding-dong doesn't have the chance to kick in with the abuse. This structure will help you get things moving right out of the gate. Like any bully, our inner critics pick on us when we're at our most vulnerable. And we're most vulnerable when we're stuck.

I'll do a quick demonstration. Udemy will be my guinea pig client. (Udemy is an online learning platform that sells courses in just about everything.) **Pay attention to how stupid simple these buckets are...**

Udemy Buckets

1. You can learn from home.
2. You can learn from the comfort of home. *(A slight word change can inspire different ideas)*
3. You don't have to go to school.
4. You don't have to commute.
5. You can learn from anywhere. *(The world is your classroom)*
6. Classes start whenever you want them to.
7. You can use the internet for something positive. *(You won't have to delete your search history for this)*
8. Learning has never been easier. *(In the olden days people had to walk through six feet of snow to get to school. All you have to do is open your laptop. In bed)*
9. It's so convenient. You have no excuses not to. *(These could be two separate buckets)*
10. You can learn at your own pace.
11. Add new skills to your résumé.
12. Learning stimulates the pleasure center of the brain. *(I could research other scientific truths about learning. They could lead to even more buckets)*

(Anything above in brackets are just thoughts that popped into my head while I was coming up with these areas. I just jot them down, so I don't lose them, but I stay focused on the buckets.)

Super easy. Nothing too deep. But my page is no longer blank. I've got twelve quick areas I can now think into. But I want at least twenty of these suckers.

Research the product, the competition, and the customer. You can also check out the client's website, social channels, and read reviews. If they have an FAQ section, this often leads to several more wells you can drill. It may feel tedious, but it will pay off.

Doing research and *"[g]athering raw material in a real way is not as simple as it sounds. It is such a terrible chore that we are constantly trying to dodge it. The time that ought to be spent in material gathering is spent in wool gathering. Instead of working systematically at the job of gathering raw material we sit around hoping for inspiration to strike us. When we do that, we are trying to get the mind to take the fourth step in the idea-producing process (The A-ha Moment) while we dodge the preceding steps."*

— James Webb Young, A Technique for Producing Ideas

From a quick pit stop on Udemy's site, I found some interesting features that could all lead to something:

13. They offer free courses.
14. Over twelve million students (cafeteria lineups must be insane).
15. Countless five-star ratings.
16. Students can rate teachers.
17. Lectures are only three to five minutes long.
18. Over forty thousand courses to choose from.
19. Courses can be downloaded.
20. You can take courses on your phone.

Twenty areas to explore, and it was pain-free. You should be able to get to twenty in an hour or two.

This approach may not be a revelation to you, and even if it isn't, I bet it's not something you're doing consciously and deliberately every time you write headlines. In fact, you may be thinking to yourself, "Hey, I already do that. I just didn't know I did that." Which is great because the difference between having a process and knowing your process is the difference between insecurity and confidence. Either way, I recommend you do this regularly, if not every time, especially if you're finding yourself getting stuck or feeling self-doubt creep in. This structure gives you support. It's not just you, the blank page, and the ticking clock.

But why stop at twenty?
What you can do next is look at what the product or service IS NOT. You do this by looking at your existing buckets and seeing if any of them have an opposite. If you're selling a fast vehicle, it's not slow. The words fast and not slow will lead you down different paths.

For example, in the case of Udemy, you could turn lectures being "only three to five minutes," into "lectures are not long and boring." These two areas will definitely inspire different idea babies.

Now with twenty-plus buckets in front of you, all you have to do is write a minimum of five good headlines under each one and you're at a hundred. It's so easy an accountant could do it.

But there's one more thing you can do to make it even easier.

Fill Your Buckets

You're now going to come up with first-thought ideas under each area. Yep, first thought. Don't even try at this stage. I'm serious. If you come up with something great, awesome, but don't force it. And definitely don't expect it. I make this point because I want to alleviate pressure and I want to ground you in reality. Getting to great takes time. You have to be patient with the process and yourself. You can't start at the end. You start at the surface and dig down, layer by layer, until you get to the good stuff.

If you happen to stumble upon something great at this stage, throw it out. No, obviously keep it, but don't stop and try and craft it into a headline. Put a star by it and keep going. You want to keep the momentum of ideation going. When you're filling buckets, focus your energy on just that.

The four streams of writing headlines:

1. Finding your buckets
2. Filling those buckets with ideas
3. Crafting those ideas into headlines
4. Editing

Each one of these stages requires a slightly different kind of focus and creative energy. When you're creating buckets, stay in that zone. Jot down ideas when they come out, but stay focused on the bigger picture. Same goes for when you're coming up with ideas. When you're in flow and you land on a beauty, don't start crafting it into a headline. It's harder to get back into the flow of coming up with ideas, and that's where the magic lies. That good idea isn't going anywhere. It's in the bucket. It's a caught fish. Gut it later.

Let's fill up one of these buckets with some first-thought ideas:

Bucket: You can learn from home

- You don't have to shower before going to school. (You can take the class in the shower.)
- You don't have to wear pants.
- Your desk could be the couch, or your bed, or the toilet.
- You'll be the smartest person at school.
- You are technically being homeschooled.
- Another excuse to avoid cleaning the bathroom.
- When you fall asleep in this class, it's in an actual bed.
- If there's gum under the desk, it's probably yours.
- The teacher's in your house. Or wherever you are in your house.
- Your cat/dog will be happy you're staying home.

If you have twenty buckets and ten ideas under each one, you'll have two hundred starting points. They won't all lead to great headlines, and several will be dead ends, but that's not the point. The point is you're not starting with a blank page and a blank brain. And if at any point you start to miss the sweet sounds of that self-doubting voice, just go back to winging the creative process.

Rinse and Repeat

Once your buckets are overflowing with ideas, dig into them, and do it with intention. Dig into those first-thought ideas again and again until you get to more unexpected territory. This extra work is the difference between good and great.

Keep wringing these areas out until you've milked them dry. Then give 'em another squeeze just to be sure. As the ideas start to flow, highlight anything you think might be decent. And again, resist the temptation to start churning any of them into headlines. Mark them with a *star and keep the idea momentum going. Things definitely get tougher at this stage, but this isn't supposed to be easy. Life's messy. Creativity's messy. Accept it. Embrace it.

If an idea or even an entire area isn't working, move on. Don't force it. There will be lots of dead ends, but they're important too. If something isn't working, ask why. The answers often lead to something that does. Once you've swept through them all, you'll have a zillion starting points, and it will be time to start writing headlines.

If you're thinking "Who the hell has time to run this process?" I'd say, "Good point!" if I thought it was. This doesn't have to take three weeks. If you can come up with twenty buckets in an hour, you could have a hundred crappy to mediocre ideas in two to three hours. Remember, this isn't about perfection; it's about getting things down on paper and giving your brain some creative stimulation. You'll have a crap ton of ideas that could lead to a crap ton of headlines.

Sticking to a consistent structure may feel contradictory to creativity, but trust me, it doesn't have to take away from the magic. A structure like this organizes all of the thoughts and ideas circling around in your noggin and lays them all out for you to see. And when you take a break, you'll have all of your buckets and know where to find your ideas when you come back to the work. In other words, this is how you can come up with better ideas, faster.

Look For Relatable Truths

When you're filling your buckets, you want to be on the lookout for human truths. These are ideas that make you think, or more importantly feel, "Oh wow, that's so true." As creatives we're so quick to rule out the obvious, but we should be seeking it out.

When I first started my career, I thought being a great creative meant coming up with something so far out there nobody had ever considered it. I soon realized it was more the opposite. It was about identifying simple, relatable, and even obvious truths. The magic was in twisting them.

> *"Dramatize the simple."*
> — Sir John Hegarty , founder of Bartle Bogle Hegarty

Think about anything that makes you laugh and ask yourself "why?". It's almost always because you can relate to it or it's familiar in some way. Otherwise, you wouldn't even notice it.

Jerry Seinfeld is a great example of someone who twists the everyday:

- "There is no such thing as fun for the whole family."
- "Sometimes the road less traveled is less traveled for a reason."
- "Looking at cleavage is like looking at the sun. You don't stare at it. It's too risky. You get a sense of it and then you look away."

- "I don't want to hear the specials at a restaurant. If they're so special, put them on the menu."
- "People who read the tabloids deserve to be lied to."

It's not your job to make the gold, it's to find it and to make something with it. And it may not be buried where you think it is.

To bring this to life in your writing, make truth lists. If you're working on something that will run during the Christmas season, list truths about that time of year. You can then ideate around these truths to see if anything emerges.

1. Every year, people are amazed at how early shopping malls and stores start playing Christmas music and put their decorations up.
2. We spend money we don't have on things we don't need.
3. It feels good to give but awkward to receive.
4. The awkward moment when someone has got you a gift, but you haven't got one for them.
5. The feeling of Christmas magic versus the reality of holiday stress.
6. Not everyone on earth celebrates Christmas. Do I say Merry Christmas or Happy Holidays?
7. What old Christmas song will be exposed as dated and inappropriate this year?
8. Someone will have to find a store that's open on Christmas Day to get batteries for their kid's new toy.
9. There's growing pushback against mass consumerism, especially this time of year (Black Friday chaos and its environmental impact).
10. How much do we spend on gifts for certain people? Are they a $20 gift person, or a $50 gift person? Or is it just a greeting card kind of relationship?

Brand: The Weather Network **Agency:** Holmes & Lee, Toronto

Brand: De Beers Jewellers.
There are a lot of universal truths in the
world of relationships.
Agency: J. Walter Thompson, New York

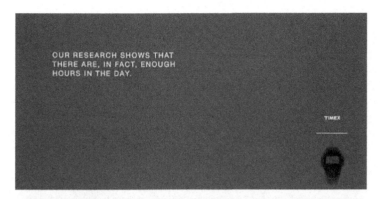

OUR RESEARCH SHOWS THAT
THERE ARE, IN FACT, ENOUGH
HOURS IN THE DAY.

TIMEX

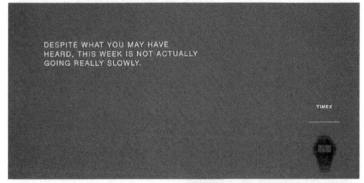

DESPITE WHAT YOU MAY HAVE
HEARD, THIS WEEK IS NOT ACTUALLY
GOING REALLY SLOWLY.

TIMEX

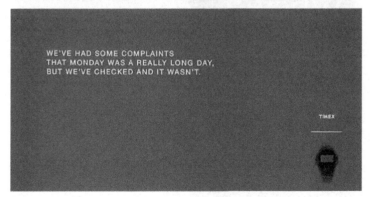

WE'VE HAD SOME COMPLAINTS
THAT MONDAY WAS A REALLY LONG DAY,
BUT WE'VE CHECKED AND IT WASN'T.

TIMEX

Brand: Timex. Classic headlines for Timex that really keep things simple. Don't discount ideas because they're too obvious. You might be discounting great ideas that bring you fame and fortune. Or just joy. Which is more valuable anyway.
Agency: Fallon McElligott, Minneapolis

Exactly how mad is she?

Brand: The American Floral Marketing Council
Everybody knows the cliché of men buying women flowers to get out of the doghouse.
The lesson here is that most creatives would avoid this territory because it's too obvious.
An unrelated but equally important aspect of this ad is that it leaves a piece missing
and challenges the reader, ever so slightly, to fill in the blanks.
Agency: Earle Palmer Brown

Where the women you hate have their hair done.

HORST
SALONS
Downtown • Minnetonka • Edina • Roseville • Uptown

Brand: Horst Salons
It resonates because it's true.
Agency: Fallon McElligott,
Minneapolis

Brand: Nike
Both suck, but I'd definitely choose a hard workout over losing.
Agency: Wieden + Kennedy, Portland

Brand: Banks Beer
Banks Beer turned an abandoned warehouse into an advent calendar where they played off a relatable holiday truth each day.
Agency: Big Al's Creative Emporium, London

What's the Benefit of a Benefit?

When you're buying a playhouse it's fun for your kids, but what you're really buying is a break from your kids.

If you've been in the ad business for more than three hours, you'll be familiar with this question, but it's a good one to revisit, even if your name rhymes with Bavid Bogilvy. So, if this is new to you, great. And if this is old to you, great. Keep asking, "What's the benefit of the benefit?" to get to the more unexpected and interesting creative territories. This question can be used to create your buckets and to fill them with ideas.

I rely on this question throughout the entire creative process. I'll ask it as soon as I get briefed (especially when briefs lack inspiration) and whenever I'm feeling stuck, which of course rarely happens for copywriters.

Let's say the benefit of the Internet service you're promoting is speed. What are ten benefits of that benefit?

1. _____
2. _____
3. _____
4. _____
5. _____
6. _____
7. _____
8. _____
9. _____
10. _____

(*Don't worry, this is the only exercise in this book, and I don't expect anyone to do it. It's filler.)

Okay, fine, I'll do it.

1. You're basically adding time to your life. What will you do/accomplish with that extra time?
2. The Call Centre operators will be so relieved.
3. You won't have to spend time on the phone complaining to customer service.
4. You'll be first up for online dating.
5. You'll catch the first wave of whatever's trending.
6. You won't have to spend time waiting for streaming shows to load.
7. You'll receive important emails before the competition (and what are all the benefits of this?)
8. You won't get frozen face on video calls. (Could be a visual campaign)
9. No more Wi-Fi rage (you'll have to rage about other stupid things instead)
10. You'll need a ridiculously secure Wi-Fi password because other people will want to steal yours. (Fun Wi-Fi passwords could lead to a solid campaign)

These were ten quick ones, but you could easily get to forty or fifty. Most won't lead to anything, but I guarantee you some will, and all you need is a few. Some products have multiple benefits so you can ask this question for each of them.

From this one question you could end up with a hundred ideas, easy. If you're an overachiever, reframe the question and you'll get even more. So instead of "What's the benefit of the benefit?" try:

What's an ...

unexpected / obvious / helpful / interesting / funny / convenient / comforting / amazing / wild / beautiful / exciting / weird ...

… benefit of the benefit?

A slight change to the problem you're trying to solve will lead you to slightly different solutions.

If all you did was ask this question a number of different ways on every brief throughout your entire career, you'd have a very successful career.

Brand: L.L. Bean
Another way of wording "What is the benefit of the benefit?" is "What are you REALLY selling?" or, "What is the customer REALLY buying?" Ask this question of every brief until you come up with something true, but unexpected.
Agency: Martin/Williams, Minneapolis

Another way to twist this question is to ask, "What's a benefit of the downside of this product?" The downside of owning a Porsche is that it's too small for your kids to fit in it. A benefit of that downside is that it's too small for your kids to fit in it. To do this, list all of the potential downsides, and then spin them into positives.

Brand: Porsche **Agency:** Carmichael Lynch, Minneapolis

Ask Questions Google Can't Predict

Piggybacking off the last tip, most creatives when given the same brief come up with similar solutions. This is because we're asking the same questions.

What separates the great from the good, or the unexpected from the expected, are the people who solve slightly different problems. And you do this by asking slightly different questions.

If you're ever feeling stuck and the ideas aren't flowing, just start listing interesting and unexpected questions about the product or the target.

For some reason, when we're focused on coming up with ideas, our inner critic is quick to kick in with the abuse. But when we tell our brain, "Hey, I'm just asking some questions. Nothing creative happening over here", it throws the dummy off our trail and lets us do our thing.

Get curious. Childlike curious. And when you're ready to get back into generating ideas, start exploring and answering those questions.

> If you want a more creative answer, ask a more creative question.

"Excuse Me, Ma'am, Do You Have Any Idea How Fast You Were Thinking?"

100 MPH Thinking is a great technique to use anytime throughout the creative process. As the name implies, it helps you spit out lots of ideas quickly. Set a goal to come up with thirty to fifty ideas in fifteen minutes. Just set a timer and go nuts. It's an exercise in quantity, not quality. Speed, not perfection. By coming up with ideas quickly you don't have time to stop, judge, and overanalyze. I use this exercise ALL. THE. TIME.

It's about giving yourself permission to suck. By letting yourself suck, you don't just shut your inner critic up, you take away all its power. Here's what Tom Monahan, the man who coined the term, says about it: *"I believe that it's much easier to come up with fifty ideas than it is to come up with the perfect idea. And I believe it's nearly impossible to come up with fifty bad ideas. And I believe it's easier to come up with fifty good ideas quickly (say in fifteen minutes) than it is to do it over a longer amount of time. Speed gives you momentum of thought, which silences the judge, circumvents fear, and makes failure less painful. Get that root canal over with quickly."*

When we stop and evaluate every idea as it comes out of our brains, it can be so deflating. Because the reality is, most ideas are bad, but you have to get them out to get to the great ones. The other problem with keeping score throughout your creative process is that for every bad idea that pops out, your brain starts to think, "I'm bad". What happens next is even worse. You stop at the first good idea because your brain is desperate to feel good about itself. "See, I'm not bad. I'm good!" And you stop there. You stop at good and never get to great.

The best creatives don't stop and judge. Don't let bad ideas slow you down. They're bugs splatting on your windshield as you speed down the highway toward Awesometown.

Bad Ideas Are Fertilizer For Good Ideas

Instead of fearing bad ideas or making them mean something about you, see them as an essential and even helpful part of the process.

In his book The Do-It-Yourself Lobotomy, Tom Monahan refers to bad ideas as crap or more specifically, fertilizer. His theory is the more crap you have, the bigger your ideas will grow in the end.

So don't be afraid to try your worst. Seriously, if you're ever stuck or just starting a project, instead of aiming for brilliance out of the gates, try to be really bad. When you give yourself the freedom to suck, the chains of perfection fall off and you get to great a lot quicker (and healthier).

And Now, Some Insight From a Former Forklift Driver

After I finished ad school, my creative genius was so obvious that my first job was in a warehouse, driving a forklift. As I loaded and unloaded trailers, I would dream up spec ads cracking make-believe briefs in my head. At a certain point, I felt like my portfolio was good enough. All I needed was an agency looking for a writer with previous forklift experience.

Instead of working on my book, I started studying the work in award annuals. I didn't just admire it; I started breaking it down, trying to extract the one key insight that may have inspired the creative. I did this for hundreds of campaigns. This helped me see what was driving the work. And what was most enlightening was how simple most of those insights were.

On the following pages, I've extracted some insights from a handful of campaigns. One thing you'll notice is that the same insight inspired all of the ads within each campaign. If you're working on a campaign versus a one-off, you're still only looking for one big insight or angle to build around, not three. It's the same idea, expressed in a slightly different way within each ad. The key is finding that big idea or insight first. And you'll know when you have it because the headlines start writing themselves.

If you're an aspiring creative, you have to do this exercise. And if you're a creative or a strategist at any level, you should too. At the very least, when you look at great work, don't just appreciate it, take a moment to break it down.

Beep. Beep. Forklift comin' through.

"I never read The Economist."

Management trainee. Aged 42.

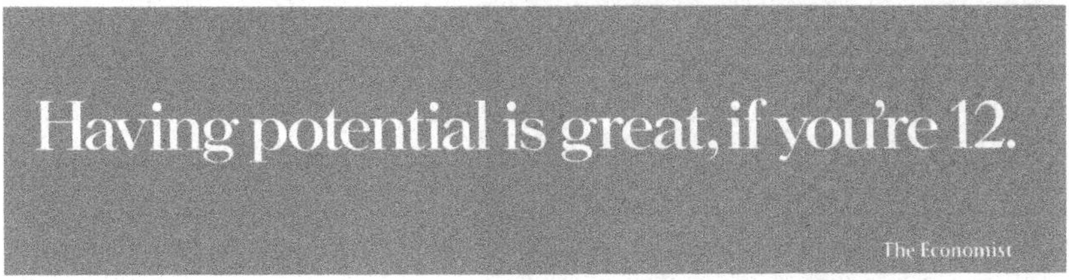

Having potential is great, if you're 12.

The Economist

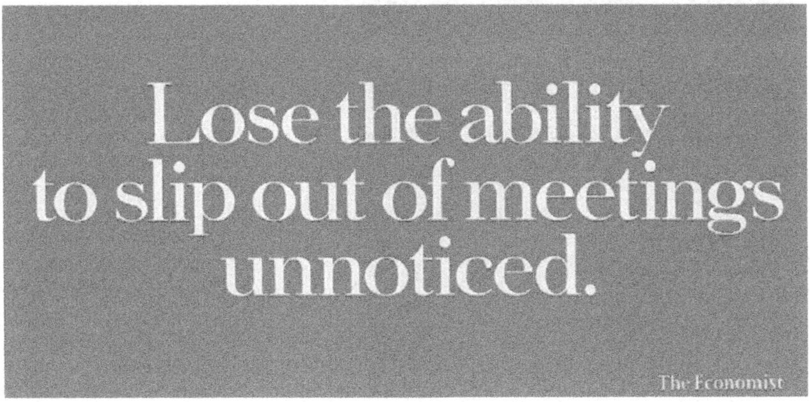

Lose the ability to slip out of meetings unnoticed.

The Economist

Brand: The Economist
Their stake in the ground was to position the publication as being intellectually superior, and they pushed it to the nth degree.
Agency: Abbott Mead Vickers BBDO, London

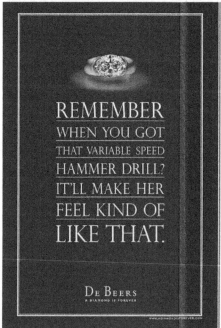

Brand: De Beers Jewellers
"Instead of speaking to the people who want our product (women), let's speak to the people who buy it for them (men)." A great insight that led to years of headlines I wish I wrote.
Agency: J. Walter Thompson, New York

Brand: Seamless
"People are proud to be New Yorkers. Let's
create a campaign that celebrates what
it means to be a New Yorker. By NY, for
NY." A clear creative stake in the ground.
Agency: BBH, New York

"You (cough) look good"

Make sure good news sounds like good news.

Brand: Ricola Throat Lozenges

This student campaign clearly demonstrates how one simple idea can inspire an entire campaign. Someone had the insight that people often cough when they're nervous or trying to hide something and turned it into a brilliantly simple series of ads. Other headlines were, "We're (cough) having a baby" and "She's (cough) just a friend".

Agency: Miami Ad School, Germany

DON'T IMAGINE A RED FLYING MONKEY SPITTING FIRE.

IF YOU READ IT, YOU IMAGINE IT.

DON'T
IMAGINE THE
PENGUIN
COMPANHIA
DAS LETRAS
LOGO.

Brand: Penguin Books
The insight that may have led to this campaign could have been, "Younger people are reading less because the world is shifting more visual. We need to find a way to demonstrate that words can paint pictures too." Copy in the bottom right reads, "Don't imagine the Penguin company logo."
Agency: Y&R, Sao Paulo, Brazil

DON'T IMAGINE THUMB-SIZED PEOPLE ATTACKING A GIANT ON A BEACH.

IF YOU READ IT, YOU IMAGINE IT.

DON'T IMAGINE THE PENGUIN COMPANHIA DAS LETRAS LOGO.

Brand: Penguin Books
Agency: Y&R, Sao Paulo, Brazil

"Bonnie, this is Clyde. Clyde, Bonnie."

See things before they get dangerous.
The Volkswagen Side Assist.

"CONGRATS MRS. LECTER, IT'S A BOY."

See things before they get dangerous.
The Volkswagen Side Assist.

Brand: Volkswagen
The thought that inspired this campaign could have been, "This safety feature helps you avoid dangerous situations. Wouldn't it be great if life came with a feature like this?"
Agency: DDB Tribal Group, Berlin

Brand: Apple
The insight for this one was that you'll be in awe of the quality of photos you can take with this phone's camera. Dead simple. Same goes for the line "Shot on iPhone." So simple it's stupid, right?
Agency: TBWA/Media Arts Lab, LA

Brand: New York Lottery. The insight for this one is explained pretty clearly in the payoff line, "What will you think about when you don't have to think about money?"
Agency: DDB, New York

EX-WIFE'S LAWYER

ASPIRINA

CAFIASPIRINA

IF IT GETS STRONGER, WE GET STRONGER.

MOTHER-IN-LAW'S CHIHUAHUA

ASPIRINA

CAFIASPIRINA

IF IT GETS STRONGER, WE GET STRONGER.

Brand: Bayer Aspirin
The simple insight may have been, "If stress causes headaches, then the difference between choosing regular and extra strength is the size of the stressful situation." Payoff reads, "If it gets stronger, we get stronger." **Agency:** BBDO, Brazil

Section II: Headline Techniques

In this section, you'll find common structures and techniques for headline-driven campaigns, and a few tips for crafting headlines.

Sack the Competition

"Find a bad guy you can beat up in the stairwell. A gracefully raised knee to a villain's groin isn't just fun, it's profitable."

— Luke Sullivan, Hey, Whipple, Squeeze This.

This technique is mostly used by the big guys, but their victims are always direct and equal competition (Mac vs. PC, Coke vs. Pepsi, Burger King vs. McDonald's). They're safe victims because they're so big they can't really do any damage. As a result, it's interpreted as playful instead of bullying. It's Goliath versus Goliath; a fair fight where there may be a few tears but nobody's getting seriously hurt. In fact, you can make a case that it's good for both brands.

But don't worry, if you're writing for a little guy and you really want to nut someone, I've got some great news. You can do it - just don't pick on a specific brand or person. Otherwise, you're a bully. What you do is create a villain that can't be harmed so your campaign is seen as playful instead of hurtful.

For example,

Coffee could sack sleep.

Vegetables could take on meat (or vice versa).

Beer could kick wine in the grapes.

Shorts could take on pants.

As much fun as this approach is, it's not something I recommend building an entire brand around. It can be effective for an initial launch campaign or a single one-off campaign to turn some heads. As long as you choose your opponent with compassion, polish those boots and get sacking.

Brand: Export Dry
Beer kicks wine in the grapes.
Agency: Colenso BBDO, Auckland

Brand: BMW. Audi billboard on the left reads, "Your move, BMW."
Agency: Juggernaut, Santa Monica

Brand: Porsche
Agency: Fallon McElligott,
Minneapolis

Brand: Burger King **Agency:** Crispin Porter + Bogusky, Miami

Embrace Your Dirt

Instead of kneeing the competition in the groin, this one's more about protecting your brand from being sacked. To do this you have to beat the competition to the punch - by sacking yourself.

What negative things do people say or think about your product? What are the most common complaints, negative perceptions, or negative truths about your product? Seriously, what actually sucks or is imperfect about the thing you're selling? Whatever it is, embrace it.

Don't worry, you've got billions of brain cells.

You can talk to your wife anytime.

Brand: ABC TV   **Agency:** TBWA Chiat Day, LA

This technique is powerful for a few reasons:

1. It makes your brand more human. Where most brands only show the world how perfect they are, you'll be a breath of fresh air by putting your imperfections on display. When you show your cracks as a brand (bonus tip...or as a person) and do it with confidence, it gives others permission to do the same. They feel better about themselves, and then they buy your pants or catnip or whatever.

2. The only people you alienate are the people you need to alienate. Your product isn't for everyone, so don't try and please everyone. Embrace who you are - all of you - and you'll attract the right people. Trying to be everything to everyone, whether you're a brand (bonus tip...or a person), is boring and unattractive.

3. It steals your critics' thunder. When it comes to your critics, it gets ahead of the crap they may think or say about you. When it comes to consumers, it gets all of the reasons why they wouldn't buy your product out of the way and challenges them to consider why they would.

Footnote

The origin of steal someone's thunder can be pinpointed to an exact moment in time, 1704. John Dennis was an unsuccessful playwright. One of his recent productions had flopped hard, other than his invention of a new way to produce the sound of thunder. While attending a production of Macbeth, they used his method. He leapt to his feet and shouted, "Damn them! They will not let my play run, but they steal my thunder."

I've heard Gary Vaynerchuk use the final scene from 8 Mile as a reference when he talks about people worrying too much about what others think when it comes to building a personal brand. Instead of hiding from his dirt, Eminem's character, B-Rabbit, embraces it and steals his competition's thunder:

> *I know everything he's bout to say against me.*
> *I am white, I am a fu*king bum*
> *I do live in a trailer with my mum*
> *My boy Future is an Uncle Tome*
> *I do got a dumb friend named*
> *Cheddar Bob*
> *Who shoots himself in his leg with his own gun*
> *I did get jumped by all six of you chumps*
> *And Wink did fu*k my girl*
> *I'm still standing here screaming "Fu*k the Free World!*

Brand: Hans Brinker Budget Hotel **Agency:** KesselKramer, Amsterdam

Brand: Roku **Agency:** Division of Labor, San Francisco

WE'RE SORRY

A chicken restaurant without any chicken. It's not ideal. Huge apologies to our customers, especially those who travelled out of their way to find we were closed. And endless thanks to our KFC team members and our franchise partners for working tirelessly to improve the situation. It's been a hell of a week, but we're making progress, and every day more and more fresh chicken is being delivered to our restaurants. Thank you for bearing with us.

Visit kfc.co.uk/crossed-the-road for details about your local restaurant.

Brand: KFC **Agency:** Mother, London

Be Refreshingly Honest

There's honesty and then there's honesty's cool uncle, refreshing honesty. When something's refreshing, it's something pleasantly different than what you're used to.

So, what are we used to when it comes to ads? Perfect bodies, perfect angles, perfect teeth, perfect lighting, perfect lives. This is why people don't trust brands. Because like most social profiles, they only show perfection, and we know there are cracks. Whether it's an Instagram profile or a product, people don't buy it. So, if you want to be pleasantly different, don't be perfect. Try being refreshingly honest.

It's the advertising equivalent of being yourself and not caring what other people think. Instead of trying so hard to impress people and wanting everyone to like you, it's doing the opposite. It's telling it like it is. It's not that you don't want people to like you, it's that you only want the right people to like you. And this matters because people relate to brands the same way they relate to people.

As a kid I loved it when Michael Jordan said, "It's not about the shoes." Everyone wanted those shoes because everyone wanted to "be like Mike." And when he made that statement, it made me want those shoes even more. It felt like someone was giving it to me straight for once. It wasn't selling me on a dream. It was selling me on a challenge. This refreshing statement empowered consumers instead of treating them like empty vessels to fill with their perfect little lies.

When you do refreshingly honest well, you earn consumers' trust. And then they give you their money.

Well, they give the brand their money. Sigh.

Brand: Oasis **Agency:** The Corner, London

"We like our clients
because of their
money. They like
us because of
our honesty."

"If you want to
double the
money in your
account, please
put twice as
much in it."

HYPOSWISS
PRIVATE BANK

Expect the expected

HYPOSWISS
PRIVATE BANK

Expect the expected

"Risk leads to wealth
like Botox leads
to youth."

HYPOSWISS
PRIVATE BANK

Expect the expected

Brand: Hyposwiss Private Bank
Agency: Walker, Zuric

Bonus Bonus Tip

A couple other techniques I haven't covered in this book are:
1) What happens when you have too much of this product, and 2)
What's life like without this product? When you dig into these,
you really want to exaggerate life with and without the product.
Go to extremes. These could be two more buckets. You're already
at five and you haven't even had to turn your brain on.

This car can help you attract women. Just drive it to places where there are women and be really charming.

The New Volkswagen up! The car that takes you places.

Das Auto.

Other lines from this campaign:

This car will help you up the corporate ladder. Just drive it to work early and work really hard.

If you want a car that lets you feel the wind in your hair, drive to a windy place and get out the car.

Brand: Volkswagen **Agency:** Ogilvy & Mather, Cape Town

Less is More

As much as I want to make a case for longer headlines, I can't. Be efficient with words. Write each one like it costs you money.

Thinking in as few words as possible can open things up instead of being a limitation. Treat this as just another tool in your toolbox. If you're feeling stuck, try intentionally limiting yourself to just five words or three, or even one.

> *"I would provocatively say to our writers, 'Words are a barrier to communication.' Not because I didn't value them - I did - but all too often they were overused to explain an idea instead of enhancing it."*

— Sir John Hegarty, founder of Bartle Bogle Hegarty

Brand: Western Union   **Agency:** Saatchi & Saatchi, Beirut

Brand: Wathan Funeral Home   **Agency:** John St., Montreal

Brand: Chipotle If you can't decide whether your headline should be shorter or longer, do both. Executed in-house by Chipotle back in 2010.

Brand: Wonderbra
Agency: Saatchi & Saatchi, Singapore

More is More

Whether it's a headline on a billboard or a social post, to accommodate shrinking attention spans, shorter is always better. Which is exactly why you should write long copy. People won't see it coming, and the shock alone may cause them to do something they haven't done in years: read. If you're going to do it though, make every word count. Edit. Edit. Edit. And then edit it some more. And repeat.

"There is no such thing as too long. Only too boring."
— Dan Kennedy, copywriter and author

This woman cooks an awful meatloaf. In fact, she is unparalleled in her ability to ruin any recipe. We make the wheelchair she uses, which allows her to get around the kitchen easily. Our apologies.

Brand: Lumex
Turning back the clock to 1993. I love it when companies, especially ones that make things like mobility aids, recognize the importance having personality in their ads. To quote Bob Thacker, VP-Marketing for OfficeMax, "All advertising is unwanted, so if you're going to crash the party, bring some champagne."
Agency: Goldsmith & Jeffrey, New York

Brand: The Economist
The general rule for outdoor is eight words or less. If you're going to recommend something longer, it had better be great.
Agency: AMV BBDO, London

MY KNEES
ARE TOMBOYS.
THEY GET BRUISED AND CUT
EVERY TIME I PLAY SOCCER.
I'M PROUD OF THEM
AND WEAR MY DRESSES SHORT.
MY MOTHER WORRIES
I WILL NEVER MARRY
WITH KNEES LIKE THAT.
BUT I KNOW
THERE'S SOMEONE OUT THERE
WHO WILL SAY TO ME:
I LOVE YOU
AND I LOVE YOUR KNEES.
I WANT THE FOUR OF US
TO GROW OLD TOGETHER.
JUST DO IT.

NIKEWOMEN.COM

Brand: Nike **Agency:** Wieden + Kennedy, Portland
Copy reads: My knees are Tomboys. They get bruised and cut every time I play soccer. I'm proud of them and wear my dresses short. My mother worries I will never marry with knees like that. But I know there's someone out there who will say to me: I love you and I love your knees. I want the four of us to grow old together.

Doughnuts are bad for you.

So are cream cakes, lie-ins and loud rock music.
So is sugar. If you take it in your tea, stop
immediately. If you take two sugars in your
tea, obviously you're trying to commit suicide
and it's a cry for help. Don't do it.
Your life is precious.

Not drinking enough water is bad for you.
You must drink 6 ½ pints a day, or you'll get
dehydrated and that's bad for you too. Don't
drink too much though, that can be really bad
for you. If you drink over 14 pints at once it makes you
feel drunk. So don't drink too much water and drive.

TV is bad for you. Watching too much can cost you
your friends. None at all and you've got nothing to talk
to them about. Lack of exercise is bad for you. But getting
addicted to gyms is bad for you too. Also, some gym
towels aren't laundered properly and spread germs.
Germs are bad for you.

Stress is bad for you. Well, at least too much stress is bad for you.
Not enough and you don't realise you're alive which is bad for you too.
The thing is, life and the living that is involved is bad for you.
It must be, because it kills everyone in the end.

At Krispy Kreme, we think the key to life, by which we mean eating
doughnuts, is balance. Sure, if you eat them morning, noon, and
night and they are brought directly to your armchair, then that would
be bad. But then if you've never felt the pleasure of eating a
delicious fluffy original glazed doughnut
hot off the line and, heaven forbid, you
get struck by lightning, well surely that
would be really bad. Really really bad.

Brand: Brand: Krispy Kreme
Agency: I couldn't find the agency credit. Maybe it was done in-house?

Current Events

What's going on in the world? Socially, culturally, politically?

If your ad is running soon, like tomorrow, you can play off current events. But you can't wait for too long. Most current events don't stand the test of time, so you must strike fast. For that reason, social channels are obviously a great place to respond or comment on current events in real time. When it comes to current events, your biggest hurdle won't be coming up with the ideas, it will be finding a client who is both brave enough and capable of approving the great ideas quickly enough.

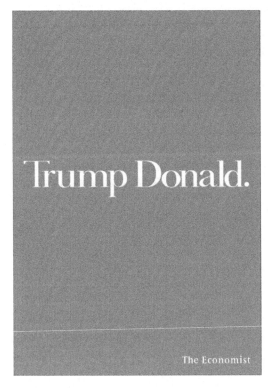

Brand: The Economist
There are exceptions. This current event headline was relevant for four long years.
Agency: Ogilvy & Mather, Kuala Lumpur

Twisted Visual. Straight Line.

If you have a strong visual idea, the payoff line should be straight. If you have a strong headline, the visual should be straight. You want to keep the focus on the most compelling aspect of your ad. Otherwise the elements cannibalize each other - which is no bueno.

In his book *Forget All the Rules You Ever Learned About Graphic Design*, Bob Gill wrote, "*Interesting words need boring graphics.*" And the opposite is true. So, if you're asked to write a line to pair with a killer visual, don't put too much pressure on yourself. Take a deep breath, and instead of trying so hard to write a clever line, the answer might be in trying easier.

Just remember:
Twisted visual, straight line.
Twisted line, straight visual.

Brand: Burger King **Agency:** DAVID, Miami

Brand: Toyota Twisted visual, straight line. **Agency:** Saatchi & Saatchi, Sydney

Brand: Guinness Twisted visual, straight line. **Agency:** BBDO, Singapore

0-100 in 5.0 seconds.
New Golf R.

Das Auto.

Brand: Volkswagen Twisted visual, straight line.
Agency: Ogilvy & Mather, Cape Town

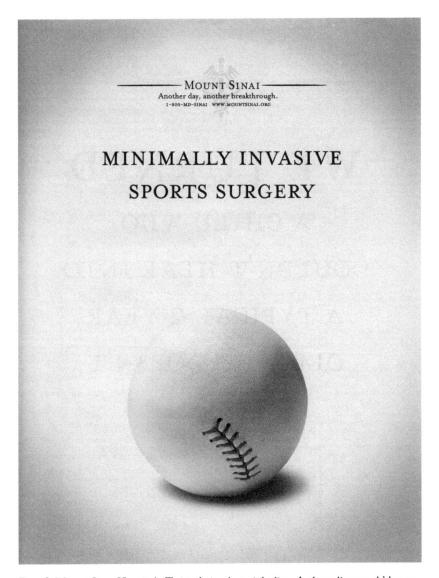

MOUNT SINAI

Another day, another breakthrough.

1-800-MD-SINAI   WWW.MOUNTSINAI.ORG

MINIMALLY INVASIVE
SPORTS SURGERY

Brand: Mount Sinai Hospital   Twisted visual, straight line. A clever line would have taken away from the simplicity of this visual idea.
Agency: Devito/Verdi, New York

Two year old Patricia Puia sat on her mother's lap, unable to hear the gentle voice that tried to comfort her. Deaf from birth, her life in Romania was lived in silence. But a month after undergoing cochlear implant surgery at Mount Sinai, the silence was filled

MOUNT SINAI

with the sounds of a world Patricia never knew existed. "I feel like I've just given birth to this child for the second time," her mother said tearfully. "But this time she hears." 1-800-MD-SINAI • www.mountsinai.org **Another day, another breakthrough.**

WE TURNED

A CHILD WHO

COULDN'T HEAR INTO

A TYPICAL 2 YEAR

OLD WHO DOESN'T

LISTEN.

Brand: Mount Sinai Hospital Twisted line, straight visual.
Agency: Devito/Verdi, New York

Leave a Piece M_ssing

Black. White. Black. White. Black. White. Black. _____?

Our brains are natural pattern completers, or rather, our brains hate it when things are unresolved and they release a little natural high when we figure something out. So, get your readers high by not giving everything away in your headline. Provide the resolution via the tagline, body copy, or logo. Or even better, trust that your audience is intelligent enough to figure it out on their own.

Leaving a piece missing is the difference between talking at someone and talking with someone. There is a sweet spot though. It has to be clever enough to challenge the reader, but not so clever that most people don't get it within a second or two. You want to make people feel good about themselves, not stupid because they can't solve your advertising riddle.

These types of headlines are usually born in the editing process. You get the idea, write the line, and then you edit until just enough has been carved away. But not too much.

> *"Keep stripping away until it makes no sense at all. Then put a bit back in until it does make a bit of sense."*

> — Neil French, Former Worldwide Creative Director at WPP Group

Brand: De Beers Jewellers   **Agency:** J. Walter Thompson, New York

KING
DING
DONG
KONG

DON'T LET THE DOORBELL INTERRUPT YOUR MOVIE.
PAUSE AND RESTART IT FROM WHERE YOU LET OFF. TiViBU IPTV.

tivibu

Brand: Tivibu. A fun little concept paid off by its tagline, "Don't let the doorbell interrupt your movie." **Agency:** TBWA, Istanbul

DON'T MORSE CODE AND DRIVE.

Jeep.

Brand: Jeep
Agency: Leo Burnett Tailor Made, Sao Paolo

Brand: Crest **Agency:** Connill Agency, Los Angeles

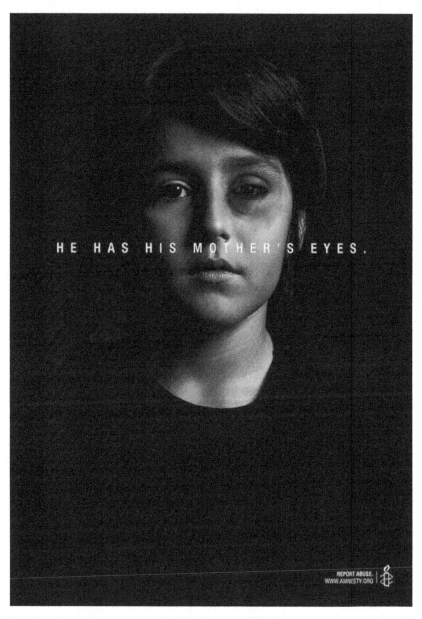

HE HAS HIS MOTHER'S EYES.

REPORT ABUSE.
WWW.AMNESTY.ORG

Brand: Amnesty International.   Brother Ad School, Buenos Aires

Manipulate Letters, Words, or Punctuation

You can

S l o o o o w t h i n g s d o w n

Speedthingsup

Break. Things. Up.

AND MAKE THINGS LOUDER.

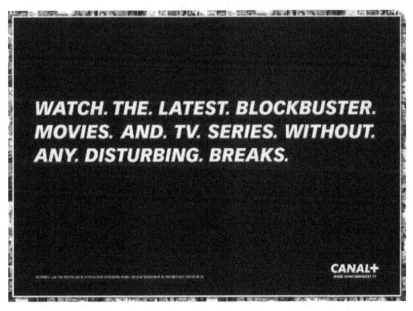

Brand: Canal+ **Agency:** Saatchi & Saatchi, Stockholm

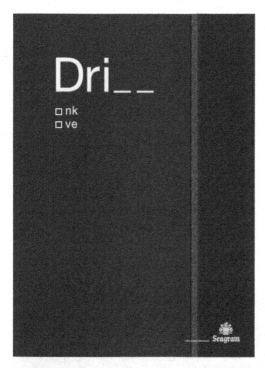

Brand: Seagram
Agency: Ogilvy, New Delhi

Brand: NFS, the Dutch Stutter Foundation **Agency:** Y&R Not Just Film, Amsterdam

Does the Product Itself Inspire Anything?

Is there anything about the product that could inspire how you write or design the ad? What does it help with? Does it move? If so, how? Does it grow? If so, where? Does it age? Is it wet, greasy, flammable, cold, warm, sticky, stinky, or sweaty?

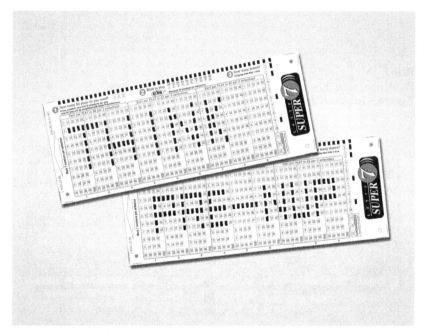

Brand: British Columbia Lottery Corporation. A little something I did with art director John Williamson. **Agency:** TBWA, Vancouver

Brand: 3M
Payoff line reads, "Post-it. Reminds you of what you already forgot."
Agency: Grey, São Paulo

Brand: McDonald's
This billboard actually grew sixteen types of lettuce in a vertical garden planted on the billboard. Over three weeks the sprouts grew to spell the two words.
Agency: Leo Burnett, Chicago

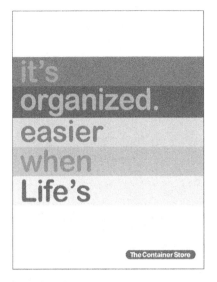

Brand: The Container Store
This campaign was done by copywriter Amanda Keffer while at Creative Circus Ad School.

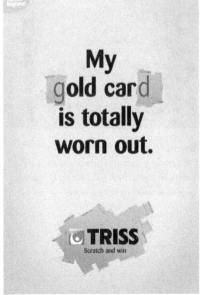

Brand: Svenska Spel, Scratch & Win **Agency:** Hollingworth Mehrotra, Stockholm

Not "What?" but "Where?"

Instead of only focusing on what your headline could be, also think about where it could be. Where's the most perfect or powerful or ironic place for your headline to appear?

And P.S., it doesn't literally have to run in these places for it to work. That's why we have those magicians we call designers and art directors.

Brand: NYC Taxi
Copywriter and art director were both Liem Nguyen. Not sure about the agency. Either way, high-five, Liem.

Brand: Oldtimer
Agency: Demner, Merlicek & Bergmann, Vienna

Brand: The Miami Rescue Mission **Copy reads:** When you're homeless, the world looks different. **Agency:** Crispin & Porter, Miami

Brand: ABC **Agency:** TBWA Chiat Day, LA

Brand: Steggles

The other examples have all been interesting media placements, but they could all work as a static image like this one. For example, just because your client doesn't have the budget to slap a billboard around a tunnel doesn't mean you can't create the image. The egg reads, "This is the only time a Steggles chicken is kept in a confined space. We have no cages, just big barns." **Agency:** M&C Saatchi, Sydney

180-Degree Thinking

In his book, *The Do-It-Yourself Lobotomy,* Tom Monahan has a technique he calls 180-degree thinking. He writes, *"Direct your thought process in the exact opposite direction of where conventional wisdom would suggest you go. Identify the conventional wisdom. Go the other way. If conventional wisdom says "soft," think "hard." If conventional wisdom says "warm," think "cold." If conventional wisdom says "low," think "high." Whatever you do, don't think of more ways to do soft, warm, and low."*

When you're doing 180s, think about what the product isn't, who it's not for, and the image you're not trying to sell.

In *The Advertising Concept Book* by Pete Barry, he writes, *"Doing the opposite is an exercise worth trying. At worst you'll produce something different and unexpected but useless. At best, it can be brilliant, inspiring, and even revolutionary."*

There you have it; don't always think so linear. Switch things up by doing some deliberate 180s and see where your brain ends up.

Brand: Allstate Motorcycle
Agency: Leo Burnett, Chicago

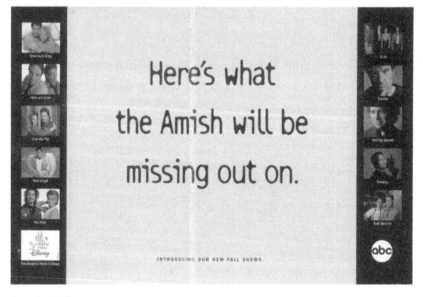

Brand: ABC
180-degree thinking is used here by mentioning who the target demographic is not.
Agency: TBWA Chiat Day, LA

Annoy the neighbours. Turn it down.

Brand: Jazz FM
Instead of thinking about who will love their music, they focused on who will hate missing out on it.
Agency: Leagas Delaney, London

Specificity

After you've written a line, comb over it to see if you can be more precise or exact with any of the details. Specificity can really elevate the quality and tone of your writing. It can make your writing more personal, more relatable, and well, just better. This technique works great for comedic lines because it tickles both your left and right brain by combining humor and unexpected logic.

If you don't believe me take it from Ernest.

> *"Details make stories human, and the more human a story can be, the better."*
> — Ernest Hemingway

See, I told you.

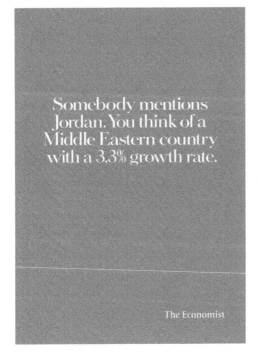

Somebody mentions Jordan. You think of a Middle Eastern country with a 3.3% growth rate.

The Economist

Brand: The Economist
For a sophisticated and witty brand like The Economist, being more precise elevates this line from silly to smart.
Agency: Abbot Mead Vickers BBDO, London

Brand: De Beers Jewellers. Variable speed hammer drill and salad spinner are way more precise and funnier than a power tool or kitchen appliance.
Agency: J. Walter Thompson, New York

Brand: Brewhouse
Here's an example of a missed opportunity by yours truly. I worked on this brand as a freelancer years ago and in hindsight, I wish I had included a specific address or email address where people could actually send money. That detail would have made this line more personal, more unexpected, and well, better.
Agency: St. Bernadine Mission Communications, Vancouver

Save the Punch for the End

Structure your headlines so the punchlines come at the end of the sentence. Not close to the end, the very end. Think of every sentence as a story. You don't reveal the big twist in the middle.

This tip is obvious when it comes to writing comedy, but it applies to any tone or emotion. It creates impact, and momentum. If you leave the reader feeling something at the end of a sentence, they'll read the next one, click through, or add to cart.

Whether it's a headline, tweet, text, or line on your dating profile, review every sentence to see if the punch can come later.

Let me try that again.

Review every sentence to see if the punch can come later; whether it's a headline, tweet, text, or line on your dating profile.

All I want is to be as happy as the men on Maury when they find out they're not the father.

I couldn't find the original meme creator, but whoever you are, send your hourly rate to dan@nelkencreative.com

Brand: Kent State Folk Festival   **Agency:** Marcus Thomas, Cleveland

Brand: Manhattan Storage does all their work in-house. In their own words, "We were the snarky Twitter voice before there was Twitter."

blake
@Leemanish   (Follow) ⌄

Sick of having to go to 2 different huts to buy pizza & sunglasses.

10:33 AM - 24 Mar 2013

2,923 Retweets   5,910 Likes   🧍🍕🧊🍩🍺🍬🍬🍬

♡ 30   ↻ 2.9K   ♡ 5.8K   ✉

Cohen is a Ghost
@skullmandible   (Follow) ⌄

most cutting thing you can say is "who's this clown?" because it implies they're a) a clown & b) not even one of the better-known clowns

3:50 PM - 12 Dec 2013

70,019 Retweets   108,623 Likes   🍀🍬🍩🍩🍬🍩🍩🍩 ।

HOW GOOD IS OUR STEAK?

LAST WEEK A MAN WHO WAS

CHOKING ON A PIECE

——— REFUSED ———

THE HEIMLICH MANEUVER.

For the very best in American cuisine come to 321 East. The food is so good it sometimes leaves people speechless. 321 Division, Elgin Il. (700)888-0612

Brand: 321 East Restaurant
Agency: An oldie but a goodie from McConnaughy Stein Schmidt Brown, Chicago

It's about as fast as you can go without having to eat airline food.

The new 911 Carrera 2, zero to sixty in 5.5 seconds. Ask for a test drive. PORSCHE

Brand: Porsche
Agency: Fallon McElligott, Minneapolis

Section III: Types of Headlines

Here you'll find a variety of commonly used headline structures. That's it. That's the blurb.

The List and Twist

The list and twist is an easy way to inject personality into a piece of writing that might otherwise be lame sauce. It's exactly what it sounds like: a list (with at least three items) where the last item on the list is unexpected or, you guessed it, twisted.

This technique is used anywhere words are found; headlines, body copy, and shared grocery lists with your partner.

Brand: Denver Museum of Nature & Science
Agency: Carmichael Lynch, Minneapolis

Brand: Target **Agency:** Kirshenbaum Bond & Partners New York

Ellen DeGeneres ✅
@TheEllenShow

Comedian, talk show host and ice road trucker. My tweets are real, and they're spectacular. @ellentube @theellenfund

📍 California   🔗 ellentube.com   🗓 Joined August 2008

It's also a popular technique used in bios as Ellen's done here.

Brand: Denver Museum of Nature & Science
Agency: Carmichael Lynch, Minneapolis

Smile Headlines

Get your straighter business message upfront and then add a little smile.

Everything must go! Except Agnes in accounting. She stays.

I also call this technique, The Mullet. Business in the front, party in the back. It may not lead to the greatest headlines ever written, but it helps add personality to lines...

This headline structure is particularly useful in three instances:

1. When a sale, offer, or message is so compelling it has to lead.
2. When you have very little time to turn something around.
3. When you're working with a conservative client (give them what they want in the first half of the line, and they'll feel heard and may let you have fun in the back half of the line).

Brand: Strangelove Vitamin Co.   **Agency:** Enigma, Australia

Brand: Budweiser   **Agency:** Wieden + Kennedy, London

Take a strong stance against
global warming.
Order some pizza or something.

Vancity enviro Visa

We're proud to support the
Gay community.
Even when there isn't a parade.

Vancity

Brand: Vancity Credit Union
Agency: TBWA, Vancouver

The Misdirect

"Once I was with two men in one night. But I could never do it again—I could hardly walk afterward. Two dinners? That's a lot of food"

That's Sarah Silverman masterfully demonstrating the art of misdirection.

Misdirection is the writing equivalent of a pickpocket. The pickpocket artist knows most unsuspecting people can only concentrate on one thing at a time. They create a distraction and the next thing you know, you're on the horn with VISA, cancelling your Hello Kitty Platinum Rewards Card.

When writing a misdirect, it's similar. You lead the reader to think things are going one way, then you unexpectedly flip the tone or message. And if you pull it off successfully, you too, can walk away with your target's wallet.

To write a misdirect, think about how you want the reader to feel at the end of the line, then start with a misleading tone or message.

If you're writing for a rebellious brand, start out wholesome.

If you're writing for quirky brand, start out bland and predictable.

If you're appealing to meat eaters, start by pretending how much you care about sentient beings. Then smash the customer in the brain with your unexpected twist and snag their wallet.

I never want children are great.

For all life's twists and turns:
Flexible financial plans.

SwissLife

You are the only woman I love a man now.

For all life's twists and turns:
Flexible financial plans.

SwissLife

Brand: SwissLife **Agency:** Leo Burnett, Switzerland

Laughter is the best medicine. Unless you're really sick. Then you should call 911.

Wednesday Night Comedies

Brand: ABC **Agency:** TBWA Chiat Day, LA

Like us on Facebook, and we will vaccinate zero children against polio.

We have nothing against likes, but vaccine costs money. Please buy polio vaccine at unicef.se. It will only cost you 4 €, but will save the lives of 12 children.

unicef ⦿

Brand: Unicef
Agency: Forsman & Bodenfors, Sweden

For hardcore environmentalists who can't stop buying shoes.

Vancity enviro Visa

Brand: Vancity
Agency: TBWA, Vancouver

There's plenty of room for all God's creatures.
Right next to the mashed potatoes.

SASKATOON
STEAKS · FISH · WILD GAME

Conserve wildlife today.
So there's more to eat tomorrow.

SASKATOON
STEAKS · FISH · WILD GAME

One of the many vegetarians
served in our restaurant.

SASKATOON
STEAKS · FISH · WILD GAME

Brand: Saskatoon Restaurant
I don't know who wrote these. If you wrote them, reveal yourself at once! One thing
I did find out is this restaurant is not in Saskatoon, which is a city in Canada. It's in
Greenville, South Carolina. Some guy named Edmund Woo opened his restaurant
and just liked the word Saskatoon. He's never even been there. Edmund, did you write
these?

For more information on lung cancer, keep smoking.

THE LUNG ASSOCIATION

Brand: The Lung Association British Columbia   **Agency:** TBWA, Vancouver

Brand: Cider Jack Hard Cider
Agency: Clarke Goward, Boston

Brand: Red Star Tavern
Agency: Borders, Perrin & Norrander, Portland

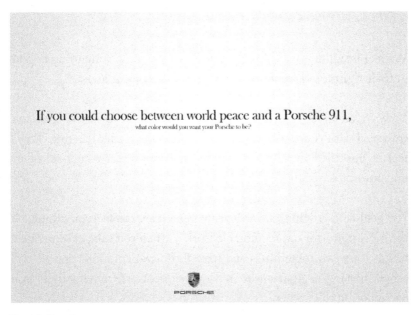

If you could choose between world peace and a Porsche 911,

what color would you want your Porsche to be?

PORSCHE

Brand: Porsche
Subhead reads, "what color would you want your Porsche to be?"
This ad never ran. It was written and designed by a graphic designer who was studying at the School of Visual Arts in New York. Slow clap for Jack Lin.

The Cliffhanger

Write a headline so shocking it causes people to do something nobody in their right mind would do - read the body copy of an ad.

To write an effective cliffhanger, make a statement so shocking or controversial with your headline, and then leave the reader hanging. They'll feel so unsettled they'll read the rest of your ad just to get rid of the uncomfortable feeling.

The goal with anything we write is to get a reader to feel something, but the most powerful and memorable work is when you can get someone to feel at least two somethings and have those two emotions oppose each other. This is what it means to move someone. You're moving them from one emotion to another.

From hopeless to hopeful.

Happy to sad.

Shocked to relieved.

Angry to guilty.

To do this effectively, it likely won't happen by accident. Try thinking about how you want the reader to feel at the end of your ad, and then choose an emotion that opposes it and write headlines to that end. This technique is all about playing in the extremes. The response you're going for after people read the headline is "WTF."

Do that and you'll leave people at the cliff's edge. But don't forget to rescue them, and quick. You're taking them on an emotional roller coaster, not an emotional ferris wheel. People shouldn't have to click through to get the payoff. Otherwise, it's click bait, and we have more integrity than those clowns. No offense to clowns

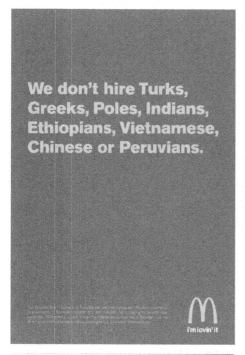

Brand: McDonald's
Bottom copy reads: "Nor Swedes, South Koreans or Norwegians. We hire individuals. We don't care what your surname is. Because ambition and determination have nothing to do with your nationality. McDonald's is one of the most integrated companies in Sweden, with as many as ninety-five nationalities working for us. Join us at mcdonalds.se."
Agency: DDB, Stockholm

Brand: Harrison's Fund
Copy reads, "Harrison, my 6-year-old, has Duchenne Muscular Dystrophy. He's one of 2,500 sufferers in the UK who will die from it, most before they're 20. Unlike cancer, there is no cure and no treatment. And because you've never heard of it, very little funding either. My only hope is to raise as much money as possible for the research scientists. They're close to a major breakthrough. Your €5 can get them even closer."
Agency: AIS London

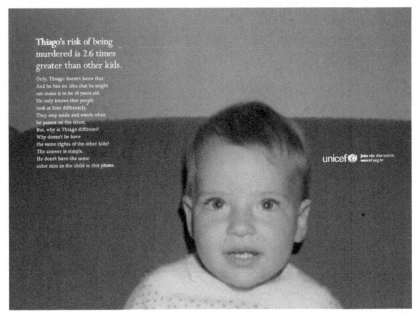

Thiago's risk of being murdered is 2.6 times greater than other kids.

Only, Thiago doesn't know that. And he has no idea that he might not make it to be 18 years old. He only knows that people look at him differently. They step aside and watch when he passes on the street. But, why is Thiago different? Why doesn't he have the same rights of the other kids? The answer is simple. He doesn't have the same color skin as the child in this photo.

unicef ✪ Join the discussion. unicef.org.br

Brand: Unicef
Copy reads, "Only, Thiago doesn't know that. And he has no idea that he might not make it to 18 years old. He only knows that people look at him differently. They step aside and watch when he passes on the street. But, why is Thiago different? Why doesn't he have the same rights of the other kids? The answer is simple. He doesn't have the same color skin as the child in this photo."
Agency: Ogilvy Brazil, Sao Paulo

Twist a Popular Phrase or Quote

If you were writing about an old trend that's come back in fashion you could say, "Out with the new, in with the old." If you were writing about traveling somewhere more mainstream versus off the beaten path you could write, "Take the road most traveled." If you were writing about a love that was a slow burn you could write, "Love at twenty-first sight." I could write these endlessly, which should tell you something. It's a technique that's very common and not something you want to use too often because even the clever ones can start to feel like a cheap trick.

If your portfolio were full of twisted phrases, you'd have a hard time getting work anywhere decent. Definitely use it, but don't overuse it. Just treat this as another tool in the toolbox and a very effective one, especially on short timelines.

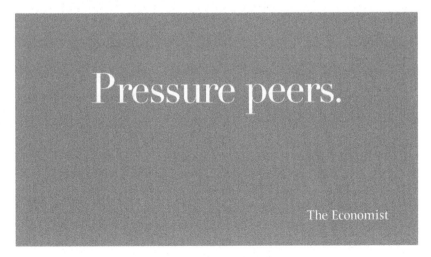

Brand: The Economist **Agency:** Abbott Mead Vickers BBDO, London

To be.

Don't make the same mistake once.

Great minds like a think.

Brand: Patagonia

Copy reads: "This spring our biodiesel repair truck will travel from California to New York doing free clothing repairs, teaching you how to fix your own gear and selling used Patagonia clothing. Bring us your tired, well-loved clothing for repair. If you don't have nay, we'll supply it. Fix it and you can keep it. Join us for local food and drinks and celebrate the stories we wear."

Agency: Patagonia knows better than to hire an agency. They keep it all in-house.

Brand: Tic Tac
Solomon Tsitsuashvili is a
copywriter who challenged
himself to create a print ad once
a day for a full year. This is one
of them.

Brand: Duke's Bread
Agency: Boone Oakley,
Charlotte

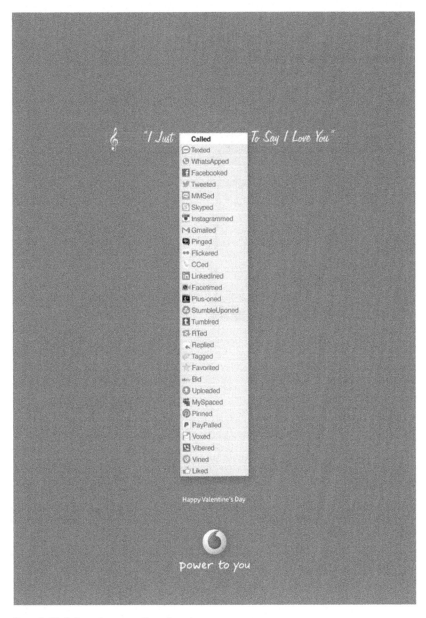

Brand: Vodafone **Agency:** Grey, London

Written by a veterinarian assistant who regrets not pursuing a career in the arts.

Personification

In a document entitled, *An Inconvenient Truth for Copywriters*, Advertising professor Suzanne Pope wrote, "*Personification allows you to present mere objects as beings capable of love, hate, fear, hope, and every other emotion available to humans.*" By assigning human characteristics to a product, it becomes more relatable, and thus, more likable.

If you want to explore headlines using personification, like any good headline, you have to come up with the idea first. List any possible traits of the product to see if some feel more human. Do any of those traits lend themselves to having an attitude or emotion? For example, if something is really spicy, it could have a bold personality. If a product has healing traits, it could be more enlightened. If a food is bitter, it can just be bitter about life. The more it's tied to product, the easier it will be to sell to a client. But of course, you can always just make things up, like maybe broccoli has a hate on for cauliflower because of something cauliflower did in high school.

A perfect tweet, even with the extra space after the first period.

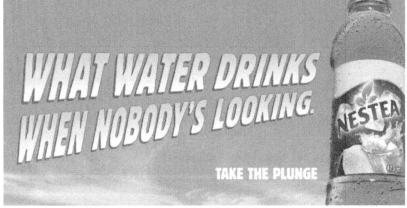

Brand: Nestea
In this campaign, Nestea comes to life. Nestea also finds a villain by kicking thirst and water in the nuts.
Agency: Lowe-Roche, Toronto

MINTS SO STRONG THEY COME IN A METAL BOX.

THE CURIOUSLY STRONG MINTS

MAKES OTHER MINTS FEEL INADEQUATE.

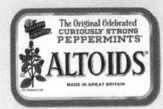

THE CURIOUSLY STRONG MINTS

http://www.altoids.com

Brand: Altoids
Agency: Leo Burnett, Chicago

The No-Headline Headline

Part of the craft of writing is knowing when not to write.

Advertising has been trending more and more visual for over three decades, so if you want to make it as an advertising copywriter, you have to also think visually. Don't limit your contribution to just words. Grab a pen and a sketchbook and draw once in a while.

In the adxamples below, these campaigns could have just as easily come from a writer's mind. And maybe some did.

Brand: Scrabble **Agency:** J. Walter Thompson, Chile

Brand: McDonald's   **Agency:** DDB, Sydney

Brand: Movistar
Payoff line reads, "Connect with your life."
Agency: Y&R, Santiago

Exaggerate the Benefit

This is a common technique used for visual ads, but it also works well for headlines. When you're exaggerating the benefit, the headline still has to be grounded in truth (so your client won't get sued) but also so blatantly exaggerated that the statement can't possibly be true (so your client won't get sued).

Before TV, two world wars.
After TV, zero.

Brand: ABC
I love when writers successfully connect two completely unrelated subjects
Agency: TBWA Chiat Day, LA

YOU MIGHT WANT TO PRACTICE
ON OTHER MINTS FIRST.

THE CURIOUSLY STRONG MINTS

Brand: Altoids **Agency:** Leo Burnett, Chicago

It gets a little bit
louder above
5.000 rpm so you
can't hear the
passenger scream.

The Porsche 911 Turbo.

Brand: Porsche
Agency: Fallon
McElligott,
Minneapolis

What About Question Headlines?

The most effective question headlines are rhetorical questions. These are questions where no answer is expected or, and this is key, the answer is immediately provided by the writer. A rhetorical question headline is one *"asked to bring your listener or reader to your chosen conclusion,"* says Suzanne Pope.

What are you supposed to do with this information? Just sit down and crank out a ton of rhetorical questions? You can try, but I don't think it would be super-efficient. Instead, once you've already written some headlines or have some ideas, try and rewrite some of them in the form of a question. It will give you a different way of looking at your existing headlines and may lead you to some gold.

Without a TV, how would you know where to put the sofa?

abc

If TV's so bad for you, why is there one in every hospital room?

abc

Brand: ABC **Agency:** TBWA Chiat Day, LA

Brand: Nike. Here's an example of a rhetorical question that gets the reader to think a little and then is immediately answered by the writer.
Agency: Simons Palmer Denton Clemmow & Johnson, London

Does anyone ever ask for your opinion?
No, not you, that guy behind you.

The Economist

Brand: The Economist **Agency:** Abbott Mead Vickers BBDO, London

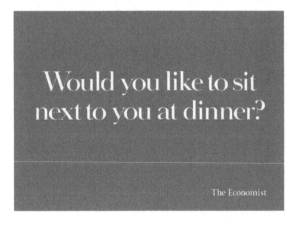

Would you like to sit
next to you at dinner?

The Economist

Brand: The Economist
Agency: Abbott Mead
Vickers BBDO, London

Last But ~~Not~~ Least, Puns In Advertising

According to Luke Sullivan, you need to *"get puns out of your system right away. Puns, in addition to being the lowest thing on the joke food chain, have no persuasive value. It's okay to think them. It's okay to write them down. Just make sure you put them where they belong, and don't forget to flush."* There you have it. Don't use puns. Ever.

Sorry Dad, but 99.9% of them are cringeworthy. Dad yells from the back room, "So you're saying there's a chance!" (Bonus points if you know what movie that's from). Yes, Dad, there's a 0.1% chance.

I'm going to go back to Suzanne Pope's document for this one. Although I know she would say to avoid them, she offered some criteria for the ones that do work. She tells this story from when she was a junior writer and brought her boss a punny headline. His feedback was:

> *"If you're going to do a pun, it has to kick both ways. What Jerry meant was that the pun has to make sense no matter how you read it. A good example of a pun that kicks both ways is the tagline for John Deere tractors: 'Nothing runs like a Deere.' Actually, there are two puns in that line, but all the possible interpretations coexist peaceably with the brand. I believe an advertising pun works best when both interpretations refer positively to what you're selling. There is a chain of stores in Toronto called The Running Room. Their tagline, 'From Start to Finish,' says not only that the store will prepare me for a race in literal terms, but also that they're the only source I need for everything related to running."*

You'll notice the two examples she used were taglines. Taglines are the one place you still might strike pun gold, if there is such a thing.

To summarize, not all puns are bad, but most of them are bad. So, flush them just to be sure.

And if you think you've stumbled across a rare one that works, make sure:

- It's a tagline
- It kicks both ways
- Both interpretations refer positively to whatever it is you're hawking
- You have other options
- Your creative director doesn't suffer from paronomasia phobia. Yes, fear of puns. It's a real thing and most creative directors are inflicted.

I'm not sharing any examples because I don't want to encourage you. Or your Dad.

Section IV: This is Your Brain on Copywriting

Tips to help you smash through creative blocks.

100 MPH Writing

It's 100 MPH Thinking but for writing. I call it 100 MPH Writing. Clever, I know.

Start with fifty headlines in thirty minutes. I guarantee you two things:

1. Most of them will suck
2. Not all of them will suck

| The best creatives fail more than the average creatives.

"Say It Straight, Then Say It Great."

— Luke Sullivan

That quote was so embedded in my brain I thought it was my line — until I re-read Whipple a few years ago.

I've probably applied this simple piece of advice more than any other throughout my career.

I use it in a few different scenarios:

1. Writing the straight line as soon as I get briefed gives me my mark.
2. I almost always get lost at some point, and writing the straight line resets my creative GPS.
3. If I can't wrap my head around the brief, I'll ask the client or the account person to write the straight line or the bad ad. If they can't do it, it becomes clear they need more time to figure it out. Beat it, suckas!

To apply this, just write the line in the simplest, straightest way possible. It doesn't have to be good. It just has to be clear. Then all you have to do is turn it into an award-winning ad.

Piece of cake.

Write. Just Write.

Take some pressure off writing the perfect headline or three-word tagline by just writing. Write an entire page. Write three pages. Write with the only goal being to write.

Whatever pops into your brain. Don't worry about cracking it. Just write. You may end up plucking a few headlines out of your long-winded ramblings or uncover an insight or two you can turn into something more.

Method Writing

If you're ever feeling stuck, or if the brand you're writing for has a personality in contrast to yours, imagine you're someone else. Like method acting, channel a character that best embodies the tone of voice you're going for and think, speak, and write in their voice. Bonus points if you can do accents.

This is also just a great technique to do anytime you're feeling stuck. It's hard to be stressed and take things too seriously when you're concepting in the voice of Gollum.

Avoid Being a One-Trick Writer

Don't always aim to be funny; aim to be interesting. Or as they say in the world of improv, "Don't aim to be funny. Aim to be truthful." I wish I'd heard this earlier in my career because my go-to was always humor.

Explore a range of emotions and styles in your writing. When you explore other emotions, you get to tap into them yourself, and you end up with a broader range of work that could lead to a broader range of opportunities.

Pen vs Keyboard

I used to only work from a sketchbook, but over time, I went full laptop. Never go full laptop.

In recent years, I've dusted off the sketchbook and it's undeniably different. Writing and drawing concepts by hand should be an essential part of your creative process. Especially for copywriters. It's so much harder to think visually when your only tool is a keyboard. When we think this way, headlines and visuals are interconnected instead of being separate elements that come together.

There's also something natural and freeing about creating by hand. It opens up creative pathways seemingly inaccessible or off-limits to the keyboard. Sometimes the ideas flow so quickly, my hand can't move fast enough.

If you're of a generation that still knows what a pen and paper are, step away from the monitor and kick it old school.

"It's just different. The connection between your hand and the page, via a tiny strand of ink, imparts something that's somehow closer to your heart."

— David Fowler, Executive Creative Director at Ogilvy

Try Feeling Intead of Thinking

Feeling instead of thinking is a great technique to use when you're asking yourself, "What's another word for x?" or "What's another way of saying x?" Instead of thinking for the answer or finding an obvious one on thesaurus.com, get out of your head and into your body. Try feeling for the answer. So instead of asking, "What's another word for speed?" ask yourself, "When I really try on the feeling of speed, what images or memories come up?"

Feeling instead of thinking, will help you come up with something more emotional than logical, and whether you're writing an ad for a hot dog or an old couch on craigslist, that's key to sellin' shit.

Another alternative to the thesaurus is thinking in images instead of words. Instead of asking, "What's another word for comfort?" ask, "What are images of comfort?" or, "When I think of comfort, what memories come up?" Or try a Google image search for "comfort". You'll scroll through images of hammocks, beanbag chairs, thick woolly socks, and wood-burning fireplaces. You'll see a cup of hot chocolate, mom's baked mac n' cheese, a hug from a grandma, or a cuddle with a sleeping puppy. All of these images should inspire something more visceral than a word on thesaurus.com.

OTHER WORDS FOR _comfort_

amenity	relaxation	assuagement	gratification	rest
contentment	relief	cheer	opulence	restfulness
convenience	satisfaction	cheerfulness	peacefulness	snugness
enjoyment	warmth	complacency	plenty	succor
happiness	well-being	coziness	poise	sufficiency
luxury	abundance	exhilaration	quiet	bed of roses
pleasure	alleviation	facility	repose	creature comforts

Headline Goes Here

You may find yourself in the following situation a number of times: a designer or art director shows you a "cool" visual and says, "This just needs a line." Or you'll get a tight mock-up with some words where the headline should be, "Headline goes here."

If I could get back half the time I spent earlier in my career trying to write lines for "cool" visuals, it would add up to a couple of years. This would be no different than you showing an art director a "cool" sentence that doesn't completely answer the brief and saying, "This just needs a visual," or drawing a box and writing "Visual goes here."

There has to be compromise in every partnership, but we deal in the world of ideas; ideas that solve problems and communicate a specific message quickly and clearly. If it's not obvious what the visual is saying, it's near impossible to write a line that can save it.

The best way to handle this is to ask them how it's solving the brief. If, after that, you think there's something there, awesome. But don't spend too much time on it if your writerly senses are telling you it's a make-work project. Don't worry about hurting their feelings. It would be worse if you weren't honest with them, for both of you. If you don't think there's anything there, tell them it's not clear and turn the page. Also, turn this page.

Microwave Headlines

"Hey Dan, you're a copywriter. What's a clever way of saying x?"

Whenever I felt put on the spot like this, my mind would start racing. "WTF! I don't have a fucking copywriting calculator, Alan! I can't write on command. I need time to properly torture myself before I figure this out! MOMMY!!!"

When you're in this state and your copywriting calculator is out of batteries, and mommy isn't answering your calls, it's nearly impossible to write or think about anything other than the heart attack you're making.

Here's how I handle this now.

First, I tell whoever made the request that what they're asking for is a microwave headline, and if they insist on something cooked in just minutes, it's not going to be gourmet. They'll get something that fills the hole and if they're lucky, it might even be good. Then I send them away. Having someone hover over your shoulder doesn't usually speed up the whole operation.

Here are six techniques you could use get to a not-embarrassing headline in just fifteen minutes:

1. Ask them to write the bad version. (i.e. Say it straight, say it great) On a short timeline, you don't have time to get it wrong. Asking them to send you the straight line, forces them to sum up their request in one sentence. If you can't beat their straight version, and you may not be able to in fifteen minutes, give it an edit and send it back with your blessing. Seriously, don't put too much pressure on yourself. It's an unreasonable request, and if nothing comes out you're happy with, go with the straight line.

2. Smile headlines

If the offer is a good one, write some smile headlines. Get that straighter, harder working message out front and add some smiles.

3. Common quotes/phrases

Rack your brain for common quotes or sayings related to the world your product lives in. For example, let's say you're selling a sporty deodorant. List any possible common phrases that pop into your head related to sport or smelling and then twist them.

For example:
> Don't sweat the small stuff...could become...Don't sweat the sweaty stuff.

Next, list any popular quotes you can think of and twist them to suit your product.

Examples:
> To stink or not to stink.
> Be the scent you wish to smell in the world.

4. Find some opposites

In the words of Thomas Kemeny, from his book *Junior, Writing Your Way Ahead in Advertising*:

> "Clients love this shit. It's cheap, but it works. Find some parallel you can make in the language between opposites. You can do this with just about any brief, any client, any offer. For example, a bank wants you to talk about their low interest rates on their platinum cards. Your line can be "Small rates. Big deal." Or "Pay a little, get a lot." If you're working on a car you could say, "Roars like a lion, priced like a lamb." Or "Giant horsepower. Tiny price."

5. 100 MPH Writing

Set that timer for fifteen minutes and let the bad headlines flow. Remember, they won't all suck.

6. Fill a few buckets

Take ten minutes to fill up a few buckets and five minutes to write headlines. Notice the ratio of thinking time to writing time. Remember, we're creatives first, and writers second.

Let's stay with the sporty deodorant example. In less than a minute I came up with three buckets:

1. You won't stink.
2. You'll smell nice. (Seriously, how dumb are these buckets?)
3. It's good for your skin.

Now I'll set a timer for ten minutes and write down ideas under each bucket (100 MPH Thinking). After that I'll set a five-minute timer to turn those ideas into headlines, which you'll see in brackets.

BUCKET #1: YOU WON'T STINK

- You can go from the gym to a date. (Headline: From working out, to working it.)
- You can go from the gym to the bar. (Headline: From sweaty to ready.)
- You can go from the gym back to work. (Headline: From weight room to boardroom.)
- You can go into an elevator without offending people.
- You won't smell like you just had a workout. (Headline: Do burpees. Don't smell like burpees.)

BUCKET #2: YOU'LL SMELL NICE

- No one will know you just came from the gym.
- No one will know you didn't shower. (Headline: No shower. No problem.)
- Outlift and outsmell the competition. (Headline: Outwork the competition. Don't outstink them.)
- Follow a good sweat with a good scent. (This one works just the way it came out.)

BUCKET #3: IT'S GOOD FOR YOUR SKIN

- Your armpits will thank you.
- You don't want rashy skin.
- Don't follow a healthy workout with unhealthy chemicals.
- No toxins. No aluminum. (Headline: Toxin-free. Aluminum-free. Worry-free.)
- You take care of your body. We'll take care of your skin.

Nothing award-winning to see here, but I have about eight that aren't embarrassing. Now choose your top three, send them off, and Robert's your uncle.

And hey, if the account person or anyone else spits out a better microwave headline than you, it doesn't mean you're less of a writer. That's like judging a dentist on their ability to pull a tooth when all they had to work with was a rock. Part of the job of a writer is not always to write the line, but to recognize it. People spit out great lines in meetings all the time, but they don't always know it. Also, non-writers don't have the pressure and expectations you do in a scenario like this, so they're loose and carefree. In these cases, it's just your job to listen, identify the headline or an idea that could lead to a headline, and give credit to whomever spits it out. "Nice one, Peter. We have our line."

One last thing on super tight timelines: the people who see your work don't know how much time you spent on something. They won't know you only had fifteen minutes, so if you don't have a line you're proud of, just send that straight line. You won't be judged for it. Nobody will even notice it, but if you send something that missed the mark creatively or isn't clearly communicating the message, you will be judged for that. Try your best, but if it doesn't happen, no big deal. It's a long career.

Sharing Your Work

If you work at an ad agency, this should be easy as you hopefully have some sort of peer-review system in place. If you don't, or you work solo, even if it's uncomfortable (especially if it's uncomfortable), make sure you're sharing your work.

Find people who are better than you are, or at the very least, your equal. Find people who are honest; brutally honest. I once had an art director partner who made fart noises when he didn't like my ideas. Brutal honesty will not only thicken your skin, it will improve your work.

When you get feedback, you'll receive helpful advice, learn what's working, what's not working, and when you're trying to be too clever. If one person says they don't get it, chances are they're not alone. I know they're your babies, but you have to get used to people calling them ugly and quickly getting over it. Use any rejection as a challenge to come up with something better, which you will.

Selling Your Work

If you want your best work produced, you're going to have to sell it. And selling it is harder than creating it.

When it comes to headlines, avoid emailing a long list and letting other people choose your best work. Have your top recommendations. You're the expert. If you just send a long list, it can be interpreted as, "I don't know what's good, so you decide." Or even worse, "I don't care." When you do this, you shift all the power over to whoever's approving the work.

If email's the only option and someone wants that long list, separate your lines by areas and insights and mark your favourites with a little star. It shows you've thought things through, and it makes it easier for people to review.

I know it's easier and more comfortable to just email a long list of lines but staying comfortable won't help you grow as a writer (bonus tip... or as a human). When you develop strong rationales for your work, you become an authority. People respect you more, trust you more, and pay you more. Cha-ching.

What do You Mean, "Work On My Craft"?

"She/he is good at craft," is something you hear a lot in the ad world. It's often said about art directors and designers, and that always made more sense. To me, it meant they had freakish attention to detail and knew loads of colours. When it was said about writers though, I wasn't so sure. Did it mean they knew what a dangling participle was? Jeez, I hope not. We're told to work on our craft, but not enough people talk about what that means. Maybe it's because they don't know either?

I used to be insecure in my ability to write headlines. Too embarrassed to admit it, I hid it. I was afraid of looking stupid. If you can relate, it might be holding you back as well. Because part of learning your craft (or just learning) is having the courage to look stupid; to admit you don't know something.

Building your craft means getting uncomfortable. It means looking at areas you lack confidence in, and instead of hiding from them, deliberately working on them.

> *"The hallmark of deliberate practice is you try to do something you cannot do—that takes you out of your comfort zone—that you practice over and over again, focusing on exactly how you are doing it, where you are falling short, and how you can get better.*

— Anders Ericsson in Peak: The New Science of Expertise

Be brave enough to admit your weaknesses. Get them out in the open and attack them. Insecurities thrive in the darkness. Bring them into the light. Like vampires, they'll dissolve into dust. It's how you'll build your craft, and along with it, your confidence.

Don't put pressure on yourself to know everything all at once. Careers last a really long time. Shift your mindset from being afraid of looking stupid, to excited to learn and grow.

Ahhh, so maybe that's what it means to work on your craft, to always be looking for ways to learn and grow. I'll leave the last word to Nike.

Brand: Nike   **Agency:** Weiden + Kennedy, Portland

Time Yourself

This one changed everything for me and it's one of the most important tips in this book. Set a timer when you start your creative sessions and pay attention to any self-doubting thoughts.

> "You've got nothing."
> "You're not a writer."
> "You're not a real writer."
> "You're a fraud."
> "Soon everyone will know."
> "And you'll be friendless."
> "And jobless."
> "And homeless."
> "You never should have quit your job as a pet food taster."

Now look at the timer. Two minutes in and you're dumpster diving. By timing yourself you'll start to see just how batshit crazy your inner voice really is. When you separate yourself from it and become more of an observer, you'll go from fearing it to laughing at it.

Other things you can measure are the time of day you're most and least creative, how long your individual creative sessions should be, how long your breaks should be, and how much total creative energy your brain has in a day. You may discover your most productive creative time is being spent in meetings. If it is, set the boundaries your brain needs.

By timing yourself, you'll also get an idea of how long it takes for you to complete specific tasks. Do you really need three days to write a few headlines? Maybe you can do it in three hours, but you have to start at 6.30 am, work in two ninety-minute sessions while listening to the YouTube music playlist Left Brain, Right Beat with noise-cancelling headphones, a thirty-minute break in between, where you refresh your brain by walking to the coffee shop to snag a matcha latte with oat milk. Whatever it is, figure out what you need and structure your days accordingly. The answers will make you a finely tuned writing machine.

MUST. WRITE. FASTER. OR. ME. DIE.

You won't die because you haven't written headlines for Palmolive Dish Soap quickly enough.

But the primordial part of your brain can't tell the difference between a saber-tooth tiger problem and a creative problem. It needs things resolved quickly to feel safe. So, it smashes the big, red, I'M GONNA FUC*ING DIE! button.

Creativity doesn't come quickly or easily for anyone, yet we don't question this response. Our hearts race and our brains blindly follow. We panic-think through the work, occasionally taking shelter in the caves of social media to catch our breath.

But we can't stay there forever. We pop our heads out, hoping the tiger's busy feasting on an art director.

Nope. Still there. Run!

Most of your career will be spent in this not-there-yet space. If you don't start calling your monkey brain on its irrational nonsense, it will make for a very long career. Or a very short one.

Breaking Good

When you start thinking of breaks as tools to serve your work rather than being an escape from work, you might start to reconsider what you do on those breaks.

If you look at pro athletes, they don't just play their sport to get better at it. They work on individual skills. They know when to train, how long to train, and how much recovery time they need. They track their diet, sleep, and energy levels. They analyze past performances and see sports psychologists. They do whatever it takes to gain an edge.

Meanwhile, professional creatives drink lattes, play ping-pong, eat pizza, show up at the blank page, and hope shit works out.

With this in mind, I've conducted some pretty extensive research. Also known as googling. And here is what google told me.

- One study suggests that the most productive people take the most breaks and that the optimal work-to-break ratio was 52 to 17. That's 52 minutes of work followed by a 17-minute break, repeated throughout the workday. This wasn't a creative-specific study or a you-specific study, but all I take from this is that breaks are healthy and necessary, as are structure and consistency. The key is working purposefully for 52 minutes, and then breaking purposefully for 17, which brings me to the next point.

- The 100% Dedication Theory is the notion that whatever you do, do it full-on. When you work, don't look at social media or check email. Work. And when it's time to stare at your phone, do that full-on as well. Separate the two activities. By blurring the lines, you become way less efficient because were you really working or were you in a TikTok black hole and calling it research?

- Several articles I found, and one Reddit post from Hanksdingdong, suggested we have about four hours of creative energy per day. If you don't believe me, or Hanksdingdong, google it. Or if you prefer, read a science-y kind of book about creativity with really big words in it. Your choice. If you're working around the clock without taking breaks, you're being highly inefficient. Figure out what your four most creative hours are in the day and strike while the ideas are hot.

- If you eat a burger and fries for lunch followed by a big-ass latte and a cookie, you're going to crash in the afternoon, be way less productive, and have to work in the evening. Eat better. Think better. I didn't have to google this one. I've lived it.

- Try and exercise during one of your breaks. The endorphins will energize you more than afternoon junk food. If a workout during the day is too much, go for a short walk. Just get out and step away from your desk. Einstein took a three-mile walk every day. Charles Darwin took three forty-five-minute walks a day. Sure, neither of them won jack at Cannes, but they did some things.

- Meditate. Do it. Your brain is your moneymaker, and meditating's like a free spa for your brain. If you're not the meditating type, you don't have to shave your head, buy prayer beads, and burn incense. Just take five minutes to shut down, breathe deeply, think about nothing, and get back to work with a fresh noodle.

I don't expect you to incorporate all of these things, but I hope one or two of them stick, and the next time you're feeling the heat on a tight deadline, they lead you to a more productive and healthier day.

Go Out on a High

When you wrap up your creative sessions, try and finish on a positive note. End on a win, whether it's one last idea or even an interesting question to explore for when you come back to the work. You want to build and maintain positive creative momentum.

Working Early vs Working Late

The saying isn't night owl gets the worm.

As someone who struggles with sleep, I don't recommend this lightly, but experiment with setting an alarm for 5:30 or 6 am, get your groggy arse out of bed, drink a big glass of water, make a coffee, and put your half-sleeping brain to work. You'll be tired, but you'll survive, and I think you'll be shocked at how productive your early morning brain can be.

If you're not the best sleeper, don't do this every day, but try it the first few days into a project or on days you're feeling pressure. When you get a head start in the morning, it relieves so much pressure because you feel like you're getting ahead of the work instead of chasing it. You'll have a ton of ideas and generate positive creative momentum before you're even at work. If your day fills up with pointless meetings, you'll know you've already got some ideas in the bag. And instead of being a sleep-deprived zombie all day, you'll be energized by your early morning genius. You might even get to shut your brain off at night. Hell, you might even sleep better.

Another benefit to getting up early is that the self-doubting arse that lives inside your brain is super lazy. While you're up working, she's still asleep, nestled in the crumbs of your self-esteem.

Step Away From the Screen

"I haven't taken a break in years!" boasts the ashen-faced, malnourished, insomniac copywriter.

Hey, I have an idea! Instead of forcing your brain to stay up late night after night, depriving it of sleep until it spits out ideas like some sort of terrorist interrogation, you may want to try, um, not doing that.

I think we put in these stupid hours partly because that's the way it's always been done. But also because creative work is so abstract. And our brains need certainty and resolution to feel safe from woolly mammoth stampedes and uncracked creative briefs, our instincts are to Krazy Glue ourselves to the work. It makes us feel like we're gaining some measure of control. It's scary to walk away. "What if the answer never comes?!" But these are just feelings, and some feelings are lies our body tells us so it can feel safe. If we listen to those lies, self-doubting thoughts increase, which can turn into panic, and over time, super fun things like depression, anxiety disorders, insomnia, and burnout. Woohoo!

Hard work and pressure definitely play a role, but not working and the absence of pressure are equally important. We have to deliberately walk away from the work, even when it feels counterintuitive. Sometimes, when it feels most counterintuitive. There's a reason people get ideas in the shower.

In the words of entrepreneur Thomas Oppong, *"Idleness is not a vice. It is indispensable for making those unexpected connections in the brain you crave and necessary to getting creative work done."*

And in the words of David Burkus of the Harvard Review

> *"When you work on a problem continuously, you can become fix-ated on previous solutions...Taking a break from the problem and focusing on something else entirely gives the mind some time to release its fixation on the same solutions and let the old pathways fade from memory. Then, when you return to the original problem, your mind is more open to new possibilities—eureka moments."*

If it helps, try thinking of your brain as something outside of yourself, like a puppy. If you continue to torture it, it will become scared, anxious, and eventually animal services will come take it away. But take care of it, and in return, it will be a good brain and help you win several Best in Shows.

The All-Is-Lost Moment(s)

You may be familiar with the "all-is-lost" moment from the world of screenwriting. It's the moment in a film where the main character is farthest away from their goal. There's no way in hell the world will be saved, and everyone's going to live miserably ever after—if they're lucky.

Its purpose is to force the hero into a decision. Give up and stop fighting or get up and slay the dragon.

This also occurs during the creative process. On almost every creative project, you'll reach a point, sometimes several, where you feel stuck. The ideas just aren't coming. All feels lost. Whenever you find yourself here, you too, will be faced with a decision.

You can choose to...

A) suffer
This is where you start to question your creative superpowers and reminisce about simpler times like when you used to work at Dunkin' Donuts. "It wasn't that bad. And the only work I brought home was filled with jelly and covered in icing sugar."

Or...

B) tell yourself you're close to something great
When you're stuck creatively (or in life) it's often a good sign. Ironically, it means you're getting somewhere. You've been to all the expected places and you're on the verge of something new.

When you're stuck, don't get down. Get determined. Tie tiny little capes around your fingers and line them up for battle on A, S, D, F and J, K, L. Then go slay that brief for Charcoal Mint Whitening Strips!

"You Suck at Writing Headlines!"

"You fucking suck at concepting! You suck at writing headlines! You fucking suck at ..." I can't remember what else I sucked at, but it was a comprehensive list.

A few years into my career, this was a drunken creative director, berating me in front of two coworkers as we were out celebrating after a presentation. My response shocked even me. I laughed.

I'd heard these things many times before. I said them to myself. But when someone else was saying them, it became so obvious how crazy, how cruel, and most important, how untrue it all was. It felt like an exorcism.

I can't explain this person's behaviour, and in that moment, I actually felt sorry for them. Only a wounded person would treat someone else this way.

So, I bring this up, not for how I was treated, but for how I used to treat myself. Pay attention to your negative self-talk. Write it down. Then imagine an insecure drunk person, or a toddler, or a drunk toddler, yelling these things at you. I'm confident you'll see how ridiculous, unhelpful, and untrue it all is, and that you'll start to laugh at that voice too.

Turn Insecurity Into Inspiration

Advice for my younger self (and fine, I'll admit it...sometimes my current self):

Do you ever feel insecure in the company of people you perceive to be more talented or accomplished than you? And instead of engaging with them, you slink into the background and try to turn invisible?

There are great mentors all around you, but if they can't see you, you're missing out. And so are they. Living in the background is stunting your growth. Don't be an extra in the movie of your life. Instead of focusing on what you might lack, shift your focus on this person's value.

When we're able to celebrate and appreciate other people and not make their level of success or talent mean anything about ours, we're more likely to compliment them, ask them questions, and then...drumroll... learn from them. I remember a specific instance where this shifted for me. I was on call with one of the top creative directors in Canada. As I was presenting, he had several subtle but brilliant suggestions for improving the work. And he was so quick. Instead of making it mean anything about me, I said, "Wow, you're so good at this. It's so impressive." I clearly surprised him. He laughed, humbly thanked me, and we both continued to work together to improve the work as much as we could.

Whether you judge someone as better or less than, neither fact changes how good you are. You're as good as you are. Better than some. Worse than others. And this will always be the case, no matter what level of mastery you achieve.

Can you be better? Yep. Are you good enough today? Hell yep.

To Make Better Ads, Stop Looking at Ads

If all you do to build your craft is stare at award annuals, it's no different than watching Lebron James highlights and expecting to walk onto the court and play like him.

Ideas come from life experience, and if your only experience is thinking about ads and looking at ads, you're drawing from a shallow pool. It's good to know what's been done, but the non-advertising world doesn't give a rat's ass about ads. They care about culture. They care about themselves.

Be curious about the world and people. Ask questions. Travel. Watch films. Make films. Read books. Reread books. Write things. Listen to music. Play music. Listen to podcasts. Make a podcast. Meet new people. Make one of those people a therapist. Exercise. Meditate. Talk less. Listen more. Learn more.

It's Only Advertising

Most of your favourite ideas will never see the light of day. And as much as I hate to admit it, whether it's the person sitting beside you or the big wig in the corner office, when an idea gets shot down it's usually the right call. And even if the reason is horseshit, you still have to learn to let it go. And quickly.

It's okay to be pissed off. It's okay to put up a little fight. It shows you care. But don't take it personally. Don't let it affect your happiness. It's not worth it. So much of this job is out of your control, and I know this is extra fromage-y, but this is why it's so important to…wait for it…"enjoy the journey."

And by journey, I mean the creative process. It's the only part of this job no one else can touch. Coming up with ideas for a living is awesome. Writing a line you love is awesome. Getting excited over ideas with other people is awesome. And when your best ideas get made, it's amazing. But if you're only enjoying that feeling and the perfect work that gets made, you'll enjoy about three hours of a thirty-year career.

Set your standards super high and fight the good fight, but don't let rejection in advertising impact your overall happiness in life. It's only advertising and there's always another brief around the corner.

Create Just for You

Most of our creative energy (and the money it generates) goes toward building someone else's agency or brand. That's why we're paid the big bucks. And getting paid to come up with ideas isn't such a bad way to make a living.

But the lack of creative freedom and control can wear on you. We have to convince, fight, and plead just to get our ideas into presentation decks where they can die because Tim-in-accounting's wife doesn't get it.

This is why it's so, so, so, so important to get your creative rocks off outside of work. If you're fulfilled creatively outside of work and you get a taste of creative freedom and control, it helps put things in perspective and the rejection stings a little less. It still hurts; just not as much.

Not having control of the creative process eats away at your soul, and let's be honest, so can advertising if you're not working with the right people or brands. Doing something for yourself refills your soul. My excuse was always that all of my creative energy went into my work and there was nothing left over for anything else. Now that I've started, I realize this wasn't true. When you create for you, it doesn't draw from the same energy source. There's this whole other tank I didn't know existed.

Another mistake I made was waiting for inspiration or passion to strike; for the perfect idea to fall from the heavens. But there are no perfect ideas. You just have to pick something, anything, and get started because passion comes from the doing. If you're a creative person, you're passionate about creating. It almost doesn't matter what you're making, as long as you're making.

Hell, if you're really desperate, write a book about writing headlines.

Find me on the socials.

Whether you paid for this book or stole it from a blind, elderly copywriter, if you read it and it helped you become a more confident writer, it's the greatest accomplishment of my career.

If you did enjoy it, please give it a review and spread the word on social. It would mean so much to me.

Direct all media things, speaking things, fan mail and hate mail to dan@nelkencreative.com. Connect on LinkedIn and subscribe to my short weekly newsletter at nelkencreative.com.

Acknowledgements

This book is the culmination of every advertising class, book, or podcast I've consumed, every creative I've ever worked with.

To Sara, my best friend and wife, thank you for putting up with me, for listening to all of my crazy ideas. I could not have made this without you. Literally. Thank you for designing it. And all of your last-minute edits.

Chris Moore! You saw something in this, and it validated this path for me. Without you, I don't know if this book would exist. Thank you.

Jill Goodbrand and Ryan Leeson, you read this at an early stage. I know it was crap but you helped make it less crap. Thank you.

To Siddesh Pai, thank you for your feedback. Also, you said your mom would be proud to see your name in a book. So, Mrs. Pai, if this book sucks it's all your son's fault.

To my Ma! You gave me the perfect mix of motherly praise and honest feedback. Thank you for always being there when I need you most.

To my kiddos, Finn and Poppy, I know you can't read yet, but thank you for inspiring me and motivating me to be better person and example.

Thank you to Suzanne Pope. An Inconvenient Truth for Copywriters helped me so much earlier in my career. It's why I've quoted you and used some of the ads you featured in that deck. Without that document, I never would have known how important it was for me to create this. Thank you for all you've done and continue to do.

Works Cited

Barry, Pete. The Advertising Concept Book. Thames & Hudson, 2012.

Burkus, David. "How to Have a Eureka Moment." Harvard Business Review online, March 11, 2014. www.hbr.org/2014/03/how-to-have-a-eureka-moment

Dave Dye. Stuff from the Loft Podcast with Neil French. July 17, 2017. www.davedye.com/2017/07/17/podcast-neil-french/

Drew, "The Creative Process", accessed Oct 27, 2021. www.toothpastefordinner.com/index.php?date=103012

Ericsson, Anders. Peak: The New Science of Expertise. Houghton Mifflin Harcourt, 2017.

Fowler, David. "Try Your Hand." The Creative Companion, undated, accessed October 27, 2020. www.thecreativecompanion.com/expert-tips-for-creative-people-copywriter/try-your-hand/

Gifford, Julia. "The Secret of the 10% Most Productive People? Breaking!" DeskTime, May 14, 2018. www.desktime.com/blog/17-52-ratio- most-productive-people/

Gill, Bob. Forget All the Rules You Ever Learned About Graphic Design. Watson-Guptill, 1981.

Kemeny, Thomas. Junior: Writing Your Way Ahead in Advertising. powerHouse Books, 2019.

Hegarty, John. Hegarty on Advertising. Thames & Hudson, 2011.

Monahan, Tom. The Do-It-Yourself Lobotomy. Wiley, 2002.

Oppong, Thomas. "For a More Creative Brain, Take Breaks." Inc., undated, accessed October 27, 2020. www.inc.com/thomas-oppong/for-a-more-creative-brain-take-breaks.html

Pope, Suzanne. "An inconvenient truth for copywriters." I Have an Idea Advertising Intellectual Archive, undated, accessed October 27, 2020. www.media.virbcdn.com/files/ba/997800ac3771eded-An_Inconvenient_Truth_For_Copywriters.pdf

Sullivan, Luke. Hey, Whipple, Squeeze This. Wiley, 1998.

Tréguer, Pascal. "Meaning And Origin Of 'to Steal Someone's Thunder'", accessed Oct 31, 2021. www.wordhistories.net/2017/03/22/to-steal-someones-thunder/

Young, James Webb. A Technique for Producing Ideas, 1939.

Made in the USA
Coppell, TX
09 February 2022

72889058R00098